THE AGILE SEC
LEAD A REVOLU

Jonna Sercom

The Agile Secret: Lead a Revolution

First published in Great Britain in 2018 by Interactive Workshops
This second edition published in 2019

www.interactiveworkshops.com

ISBN 978-0-244-43450-2

Editor: Victoria Lympus
Proofreader: Stephanie Sercombe
Designers: Chris Lissaman, Matteo Bisato, Rosie Blyth

CONTENTS

INTRO

It's on. That's the first thing. This revolution is definitely on. We are living in the age of revolutions: #trump, #Brexit, #metoo. I first became aware of the thermonuclear power of social media during the Arab Spring. Something was happening. Tech inspired. But to do with people.

You could say the seeds of the revolution were sown at the end of the 1980s and with the death of the yuppie. You could say it was born during the global financial crisis and its messy aftermath.

All revolutions begin with dissatisfaction. But what were we so dissatisfied with? How did a revolution start without us knowing? With so few realizing? It seems we got frustrated going to work and being evaluated on presenteeism. And we wanted to trade all that for the satisfaction that comes from making something. As our status-consciousness decreased, we no longer cared about making Senior VP. As pension regulations changed, there was no cash incentive to suck up 20 years of boredom. What do we want: Interesting work! When do we want it? Now!

Putting things very simply: Just as the industrial revolution attracted peasant farmers and the self-employed skilled workers into factories, so the tech revolution has enabled those workers to head back home. And in exactly the same way that large factories required all workers to be present at the same time, working as hard as possible, so today's freelance workforce has realized, "Hey, I don't need to be in that team meeting. I can be at the beach. Or wherever I want to be. You don't own me."

In 2001, pioneers in the tech industry assembled to debate a simple question. Why were their projects failing? Overrunning. Cost issues. Unhappy clients. The solution was a new methodology: Agile.

Yes, agile is a buzzword. But, first and foremost, agile is a methodology. Agile is a completely different way of getting things made. And, if it's a different way of getting things made, for many of us, agile is a different way of doing our working life.

Here is the secret: Shhh … Without even doing agile we can extract its essential goodness, and inject it to supercharge our mindsets, culture, leadership and working style.

Combine completely different labour-market drivers with a completely different way of doing work and what do we get? Well, a completely different way of running businesses, departments and teams. A new ethos.

The rise of agile and the freelance revolution therefore requires a completely different way of running teams. *Running* teams, rather then leading teams. We can argue the point, but broadly this new leadership is "hands-on-hands-off". It's an energizing, crazy, bottom-up, outcome-focused riot of productivity where only the best survive.

In three simple chapters, we will explore:

// Five factors powering the revolution
// The Agile Manifesto: How to get the most done in the least amount of time
// The Agile Leadership Manifesto: How to lead teams that ship enormous amounts of work easily.

Does anyone really read a book right through? I don't. So:

Dip into Chapter One: If you are fascinated by cultural changes and drivers and want to explore things more philosophically. This is the rationale, the foundations.
Dip into Chapter Two: If you want to understand a better way to do nearly everything. A step-by-step guide to the key tenets of productive, engaged teams.
And dive deeply into Chapter Three: If you want to understand what we, as leaders, can do to create and lead extraordinary teams.

AGILE MANIFESTO

1

Our highest priority is to satisfy the customer through early and continuous delivery of valuable things.

2

Welcome change requests, even late in projects. Agile processes harness change for the customer's competitive advantage.

3

Deliver working products frequently, from a couple of weeks to a couple of months, with a preference for the shorter timescale.

4

Business people and developers must work together daily through the project.

5

Build projects around motivated individuals. Give them the environment and support they need, and trust them to get the job done.

6

The most efficient method of conveying information to and within a team is face-to-face conversation.

7

Working products are the primary measure of progress.

8

Agile processes promote sustainable workrates.
The sponsors, developers and users should be able to maintain a constant pace indefinitely.

9

Continuous attention to technical excellence and good design enhances agility.

10

Simplicity – the art of maximizing the amount of work not done – is essential.

11

The best architectures, requirements and designs emerge from self-organizing teams.

12

At regular intervals, the team reflects on how to become more effective, then tunes and adjusts its behaviour accordingly.

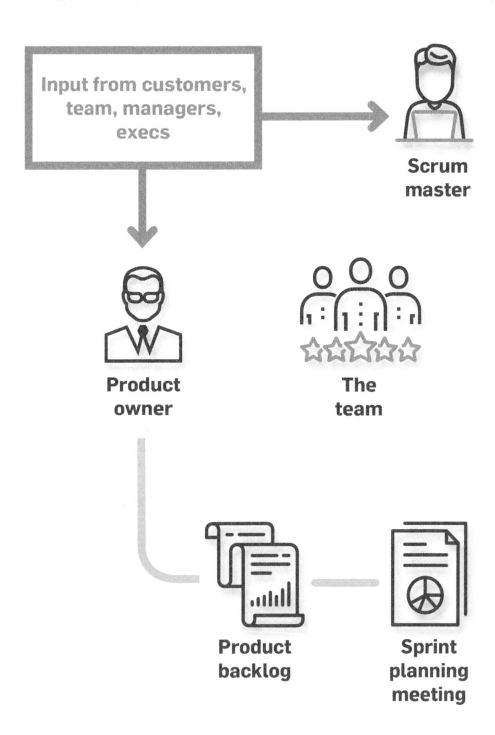

Input from customers, team, managers, execs

Scrum master

Product owner

The team

Product backlog

Sprint planning meeting

AGILE PROCESS

Daily standup meeting

1-4 week

Sprint review

Sprint backlog

Sprint retrospective

CHAPTER 1

CONDITIONS FOR THE REVOLUTION

LIVING IN THE VUCA WORLD

The VUCA world is: Volatile, Uncertain, Complex, Ambiguous. It is a term that was first coined by the US military in 1987.

In 2000, organizations and governments were still broadly operating on the basis that the future would unfold in a predictable, stable, linear fashion. Politics was still, to some extent, ideological. The economy was growing in a linear fashion. Radical extremism was a third-world problem. And corporates were the temple of capitalist religion.

We could not have seen that within 20 years: Terrorism would repeatedly strike Europe; we would experience a decade of low/no growth; migration would lead to populism; Putin would be active in the Balkans; Trump would pull America back from the global stage; Brexit; the eurozone crisis; Greece would become a second-world country and Italians would vote to "rid themselves of hostile German financial control". We cannot predict the world in 2040.

So what does this mean for customers? Well, it means that big decisions are very hard to make. The radical thinking that led to, say, the beautiful Airbus A380 may still be relevant. But the appetite in customer groups to make such decisions will be lacking.

The UK government's strategic defence review in 1998 estimated the cost of replacing the UK's nuclear submarines at £12 billion. It was only finally approved in 2016 after 18 years of decision-making. The growing cost of those submarines by 2018 was considered to be £31 billion. Is there really an ongoing appetite in governments for this type of decision-making if they could have an alternative?

In a VUCA world, customers want to make the smallest possible decision, as late as possible.

We are the Amazon generation. We are used to deciding today, to have it tomorrow. Political, economic and social pressures mean long-term decisions are difficult to make. Every big decision is subject to constant review and a large amount of pressure. We are, at heart, still just a consumer generation. Let me decide what I want now. Don't make me wait.

To avoid making decisions, there's a new way of living: Let me be a subscriber.

Here is a list of things our company subscribes to:

// All our email
// All our data storage
// All our finance software
// All our finance expertise
// All our sales software
// All our project-management software
// All our desks, buildings and infrastructure
// Our board governance
// Half our people

The subscriber model allows us to decide on a month-by-month basis what we want, and pay for it on a contractual basis. This is the ultimate strategy in a VUCA world. If the world changes tomorrow, we change with it. Scale up, scale down; premium version in good times, basic in others. When customers get used to subscription models in their private life, subscription becomes accepted in their work lives.

WeWork is a subscription-based, per-desk office space, based on monthly contracts. We recently upgraded our accounting subscription to top-four global accounting firm Deloitte. And where did these supposedly conservative, traditional, cautious people want to meet us? WeWork.

Customer organizations are asking, "What is the job that needs doing here?" And, "What's the easiest way to get this done with the lowest risk?"

In VUCA subscriber land, customers ask, "Is there any other way I can get that job done?" I can get to work by Mobike, tube or Uber and I can pay 50p, £1.50 or £5 for these. British weather is pretty much VUCA. So I can adapt. Cheap when the suns out. Splash out when it rains. And the maths stacks up.

When I do the school run, Uber costs £5. If I drive, parking costs £1. And my car depreciates at a rate of about £10 per day. Plus I have to pay for fuel (£4), tax (£1) and insurance (£2). Why am I going to pay £18 to do a job I can get done for £5? Take the driver out of the equation and we are looking at less than £2 to do the job.

VUCA-world citizens embrace subscription. And that's why VUCA-world citizens love the freelance revolution.

THE FREELANCE REVOLUTION

When I first sat down on the fourth floor of a rented apartment in West London on a sunny October morning in 2005, I had no idea if this was going to work. I'd been a good corporate citizen. I'd done my degree. Completed my graduate scheme. Worked hard on my executive path to reach a managerial role inside the first five years of my big, fat corporate job. Then I went out and got a job agency-side, utilizing my psychological training in a product-design role.

I'm not sure if I was freelance completely of my own free will. The CEO had taken umbrage with me going to a wedding in Scotland for the weekend rather than sitting at home dealing with his last-minute change of scope. When I got back from the wedding my boss tried to give me a "verbal warning". I just point-blank handed in my notice. Busting your balls for someone who throws that kind of stuff around is one of the major downsides of corporate life. I worked my notice and gave myself three months to freelance and see what happened. With no kids and no mortgage, I only needed to clear a grand a month and I could make my rent. So I sat with an empty diary enjoying the view. The phone rang. "Can you deliver a two-day stress-management course in Holland next week for £400 per day?" "No stress. Yes!"

I can say with some certainty, because I was there, that the employment world in the early 2000s was dominated by the belief in corporations. We wanted those jobs. We aspired to fixed, permanent contracts. Company cars. We anticipated long careers. We didn't know then that it was the end of a paradigm from the 1980s.

Now, a radically different paradigm exists. Accurate stats for the Eurozone are notoriously hard to put together, but in the US there are now more than 53 million freelancers: 34% of the workforce, contributing approximately $715 billion to the economy. Of those freelancers, 77% say the best days of freelancing are ahead. In the UK, 87% of graduates with a first- or second-class degree consider freelancing a highly attractive or lucrative career option, and 29% say freelancing is part of their career strategy in the next five years.

In the EU, freelancing has increased by 45% in four years, making it the fastest-growing labour market. Official reporting of these statistics also underrepresents this workforce. In Spain, for example, official research shows a proportion of 15% of freelancers, whilst McKinsey's own research yields a figure near to 25%.

But what do these freelancers want? It's not responsibility. It's not recognition. Just like an Uber driver, or me sat in my apartment in 2005: "Give me a defined deliverable and pay me to do it. That's it. Don't put me in a hierarchy. Don't make me go to lots of meetings. Don't offer me fancy promotions. Don't try to tie me in. Just decide what you want done. And pay me to do it." How can complex organizations compete with an employment form that says, "You decide when you work, where you work, for whom you work, what you get paid and, by the way, there will be no hierarchical pain, no HR and very limited organizational friction"?

So, instead of spending time stuck in meetings or having your annual appraisal, why not go to the beach or wherever you choose. What we didn't know in 2000 is that, whilst the industrial revolution moved much of the workforce from self-employment to structured payroll jobs, now the digital revolution is creating a shift in the opposite direction. UK predictions are that 50-80% of the workforce will be freelance by 2050.

London freelancer's start-up YunoJuno, run by my good friend Shib Matthew, is an example of an organization that has exploited the disruption of freelance. YunoJuno matches tech freelancers with corporations doing projects. YunoJuno have 15,000 freelancers on their platform, from 30,000 who have applied. These are highly skilled workers, doing complex and high-value jobs.

The highest-paid freelancer on the YunoJuno platform made over £250,000 in a year. These are not crap jobs.

Freelancing is a seismic change. But one that complements agile – which involves breaking down complex problems into small problems, solved in sprints – perfectly. By adopting agile methods and culture, we can place these projects onto the relevant subscription platforms or with the most suitable freelancers and have them solved.

The freelance revolution is also a mechanism that enables large amounts of parallel working. Because resources are scalable, everything can be worked on at the same time.

Organizations that will succeed in the next 20 years will be masters of freelance. And for successful freelance, we need digital.

For successful freelance, we need digital.

THE DIGITAL
REVOLUTION

Stumbling down the road, mid weekend, it's quite easy
to dip into a WhatsApp and keep up with a bit of work.
Whatever people tell you, it's not hard. It's not a trouble.
In fact, it's normally quite fun. And you get a tiny hit of
dopamine by ticking something off your to-do list. No-one
ever stumbled into a car factory for five minutes at the
weekend and dipped into a production line. And if they
were called in, well, then there was overtime.

The digital revolution has reversed 200 years of work trends.
Industrialization drove itinerant peasant farmers into urban
factories. The idea that machines might take over has existed
for a very long time. AI is the next great wave of this concern.
Both physical machines and computers have taken the grunt
work out of a great deal of life.

New freedoms have emerged. The freedom to connect when
and wherever. The freedom to work at times that work for
us as individuals. The freedom to shape work back around
life, rather than life around work. This culture has prevailed
in many parts of the world. Rural France still knocks off for
lunch and closes the shop. And rural anywhere has children
integrated into the day, whether because teenagers need a lift
or because footfall in the mom-and-pop store allows some
connection to the family home. We are beginning to create
urban versions of ancient rural life.

Co-working spaces are springing up, a semi-formal
acknowledgement of the fluidity of our current practice. And
campus workplaces have, for a couple of decades, replicated
the sense of the living–learning life of university. Digital has
driven this fluidity deeper.

But work itself has also dramatically changed. Knowledge workers, by definition, are doing something with their mind, not their hands. Service economies, like the UK, therefore have no barrier to fully digital homeworking.

Face-to-face is still a priority at times. But face-to-face is not essential. In fact, it raises a big question: If we are going to offices, what are we going for? Logically speaking, we are going to achieve something. What are we there to achieve? Let's look at what we don't want to achieve:

// Pointless meetings
// Getting annoyed by our boss
// Hours of email
// Fiddling with Excel
// Working on a presentation
// Research

All these things can be done from home. Or, better, not done.

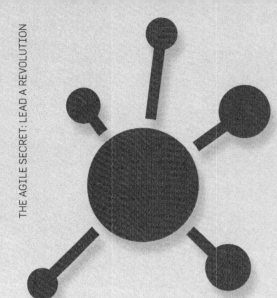

Part of why we are going is to belong. Therefore, meaningful conversations, connection, support and advice are all important. So is social time. In our office, we have three daily social spots: Mid-morning matters, lunch and high tea.

Socializing is not the main reason we are at work. We are there to do something. Something productive. One workshop participant attending a seminar we ran on this summarized it well: "So you are saying ... makings not meetings."

"Makings not meetings" has become our team mantra. Broadly, we work for makings. Presentations. Excel. A research document. In the language of project management, we are here not for deliverables on a work-breakdown structure, but to achieve deliverables on a product-breakdown structure. Whilst a work-breakdown structure calculates the effort put in, a product-breakdown structure calculates the products produced.

In a knowledge economy, with tech enabling play and work anywhere, the fascinating thing is that we have come almost full circle – the equivalent to hammering out a horse shoe on an anvil. Whilst hitting that Mac keyboard, in essence, we are producing an artisan bit of copy/graphics/code/financial advice. We have become again the rural harvesters turning our hands to what needs done as close to home as possible.

We have become again the rural harvester turning our hands to what needs to be done as close to home as possible.

THE BIRTH OF AGILE

People who meet in a place called "Snowbird, Oregon" are probably already quite cool. The 17 people in Snowbird on 11 February, 2001, had come because of an email. In September, 2000, Bob Martin from Object Mentor in Chicago wrote to a few tech insiders:

I'd like to convene a small (two-day) conference in the January to February 2001 timeframe here in Chicago. The purpose of this conference is to get all the lightweight method leaders in one room. All of you are invited; and I'd be interested to know who else I should approach.

"Lightweight" was the working title for all the software development methodologies of the time that tried to step outside of the established "waterfall" method.

At the Snowbird meeting, these gurus batted around how they could escape corporatism, legal wrangles and frustration with bosses because software development was behind schedule.

They started by writing down a few simple bullet points:

//   Insist on feedback
//   Collaborate openly and continuously
//   Work at a sustainable rate
//   Work only to produce business value
//   Understand the roles of the business and developers
//   Commit

After lunch, Martin Fowler and Dave Thomas started to work out a format for expressing these pithy statements. They came up with the following: "We prefer X over Y."

As the rest of the group drifted back after lunch and into the afternoon they had come up with four bullets, plus an introduction:

"We are uncovering ways of developing software by doing it and by helping others to do it. We value:

//   Individuals and assertions over process and tools.
//   Working software over comprehensive documents.
//   Customer collaboration over contract negotiation.
//   Responding to change over following a plan."

This group called themselves "The Agile Alliance" and tagged their bullets "Manifesto for Agile Software Development".

As my wheels touched down at Airbus HQ in Toulouse for a client meeting 17 years later, I could see over a security fence that the Snowbird group's impact had gone way beyond software. We were meeting to discuss a keynote for some of Airbus's top military brass. And waiting for me on the runway was the latest Airbus Beluga XL. The Airbus executives shared with me that this plane had been built using agile methodologies, reducing the work done by around 30%. On a plane whose development costs were around a billion euros, that's quite a saving.

Way beyond software, a whole crew of aerospace engineers have used this simple manifesto to produce a highly complex physical thing. And if we can make one of the world's biggest planes in an agile way, surely we can use it for pretty much everything in between? Is there seriously anything that doesn't work in agile?

If this is the case, the next question to ask is: How?

// How can we do agile in different sectors?
    In banking, property, law, engineering, marketing?
// How can we do agile across functions?
    In accounts, HR, procurement, sales?
// How can we do agile in individual roles? As a team assist,
    a front-office financial expert, a leader?

In our company, the breakthrough came when we had large amounts of written documents to create as part of designing a workshop. We realised that one person working through all these over a number of weeks had none of the excitement and urgency of a short-term blast. With barely any knowledge of agile we created our own rules for what we call a "hack":

1. We are doing nothing else. No phones. No emails.
2. Keep it short. Max two days. Ideally, one.
3. Hacks are not for strategy. They are for deliverables.
4. We must have a very clear list of deliverables at the
    start, including exact spec.

And we borrowed something I've always loved from the way the Catholic Church selects a pope.

5. No-one leaves until all the work is finished.

It worked. But why? Well, we had restored something that has been lost in the age of email. Something so powerful that it drives us every day. Something so simple, so addictive, we can crave it like a drug. We had re-harnessed the pure, adrenaline-fuelled, serotonin-boosting, flow-capturing beauty that is *urgency*.

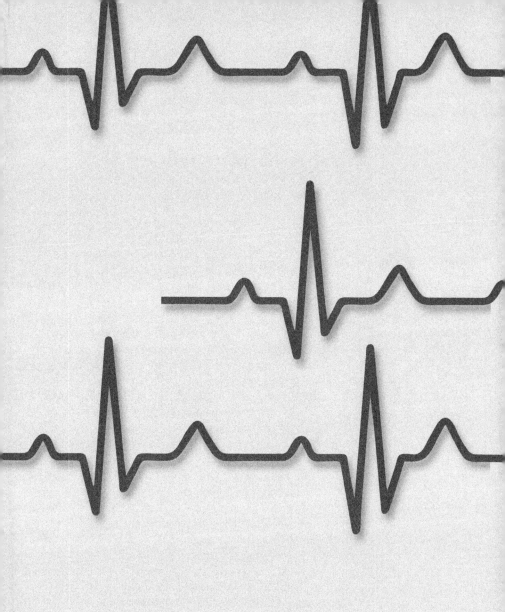

THE POWER OF URGENCY

Just do it. The power of now. A goal is a dream with a deadline. Why put off till tomorrow what you can do today?

There's something hard-wired into the human brain and nothing that focuses human effort more than time pressure. Something primeval within us knows that a clock is ticking, the world spinning, time marching on. We had better do the important things and we had better do them now.

Exactly what that thing is varies by month, person, life-stage. Some of us are desperate to start a family. Others to get through the month end. Others, like Usain Bolt, to hit the finish line less than ten seconds after leaving the start line, but before anyone else. Whilst, of course, true Zen masters know there is nothing but the present moment, the rest of us are just trying to get on with stuff.

Urgency is what drives us to try to win wars before the winter, build companies before the VC dries up, buy houses whilst interest rates are low, lose weight before the wedding. For those of us looking for commercial advantage, we know we can only be first if we are also fastest.

In the VUCA world, decisions are hard. Those Snowbirds knew it. They were facing the effects of highly complex, difficult decisions, in changing and ambiguous circumstances. They did what we all do if we can. They started pursuing simplicity.

They asked questions we could all consider:

// What can we make today?
// What can we finish this week?
// How can we break things down into simple products or components and deliver them in a very short timeframe?

Priority means to come earlier in time or sequence. Those software guys asked a very simple question: What comes first?

We can make our own VUCA worlds if we drag projects out over months, book endless complex client meetings, engage with multiple stakeholders. But the freelance revolutionary knows their income depends on clarity of mind and purpose. Dedicating effort to the job in hand.

So let's take a single item or deliverable, and make it urgent. And then let's dedicate every bit of effort to finishing it as quickly as possible. Urgency helps us make good decisions about what compromises to make along the way. It helps us avoid the unnecessary feature or conversation. It helps us achieve our outcome.

Consider these two questions:

1. What would you do if you wanted to change the world in a lifetime?
2. What would you do if you wanted to change someone's life in the next ten minutes?

The first question may well get the best yield. It also has the biggest risk. We admire the ambition of people who want to do the former. But we love the pragmatism of the people who can do the latter. (In fact, if you want to do the latter, you can simply log-on to compassionuk.org and sponsor a child in poverty. That's what I would do. That's what I've done.)

Focusing on things we can do now reduces decision-making complexity. It de-conflicts priorities. Making things urgent gives us a payoff today. It's done. Signed. Sealed. Delivered.

There's a certain pride in saying the words, "It is finished."

Getting stuff done today gives us personal satisfaction, too. Our confidence builds because we've achieved something. Every day at Interactive Workshops, we start a meeting at 9:06 am for a maximum of ten minutes. Nicknamed "Office Awesome", we each identify three things we will deliver that day. And, by the way, meetings don't count. Email doesn't count. Conversations don't count. Building strategies doesn't count. Management doesn't count. This short conversation flexes the deadline muscle. Ticking off tasks gives us the completion reward. Built into agile is this gorgeous short-term cycle of productivity, delivery and feedback.

Try living like this for a few weeks and life somehow becomes more effortless. More enjoyable. Partly because delivering builds self-confidence. Partly because it wins the buy-in of others.

Try working like this in a team and we can create a can-do unit of go-to winners. Responding positively to urgency builds supreme confidence in the group. The shared cohesion adds an extra layer of resilience. Then, when the storm comes and the whole team is under pressure, they already believe they have the power to get it done.

Urgency also allows us to do things that are "good enough". Technically, this could be called a "minimum viable product". Psychologists call this "satisficing". Urgency helps counter the ego-driven perfectionism that makes us want only to do the very best.

People hate this. But compare Obama's and Trump's presidencies. Obama laid out great plans and is a *truly wonderful person*.* He achieved a great deal. But Trump has the edge on identifying an issue, and then poking it with a stick until it's done. What Trump knows, which Obama only later realized, is that getting something done today often beats

*I've inadvertently used a Trump soundbite.

getting the best thing done down the line. Please never make me speak on the US East Coast about this. I would not vote for Trump. Merely commenting on the approaches of these two ridiculously different men who have both run the most powerful country in the world.

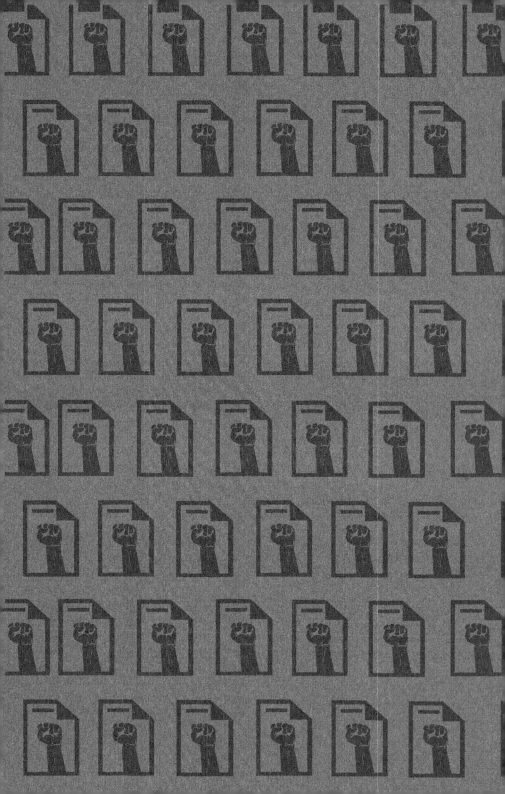

CHAPTER 2

THE AGILE MANIFESTO

GET IT DONE

Agile Manifesto Rule #1: Our highest priority is to satisfy the customer through early and continuous delivery of valuable "things".

Let's dissect this rule:

Let's dissect this rule:

Stop.

Let's dissect this rule:

Let's dissect this rule:

clause | interpretation

clause	interpretation
Our highest priority	pretty unequivocal
Is to satisfy the customer	sketchy ... satisfy? **sat·is·fy** Latin **satis (enough)**, Latin **facere (make)** → Latin **satisfacere (to content)** → Old French **satisfier** → Late Middle English **satisfy** Ok. Make enough to make someone content.
Through the early and continuous	Early? I love that. My management 101 tip for all people everywhere is to get their work done early. But early and continuous? Keep doing it early. Wow. That's going to make people pretty happy.
Delivery of valuable things.	Delivery of valuable things. Valuable by definition means it's good.

THE AGILE MANIFESTO

35

When we started Interactive Workshops, my buddy Andy and I settled on three maxims. Below are the benign, non-motivating, PG versions:

1. Get it done.
2. Don't mess up.
3. Say yes first, then work out how afterwards.

I've recently been on-boarding a new hire, Chris. He's a great guy. Taking a crisp piece of paper, I explained really clearly the huge benefit of getting his most important work done Monday through Wednesday. Leaving important stuff to Friday just means we lose both contingency and peace.

Built into the Agile Manifesto Rule #1 then, is a mechanism to make this customer pretty happy. If they get good-enough stuff early, and all the time, they are going to be pleased. Notice they haven't got everything. It's not perfect (unless perfect was part of the good-enough criteria). Imagine you go to a sandwich shop and they consistently make you a fully satisfying and delicious sandwich that is always ready just before you expect. Mmmm...

Back in the real world, a bunch of individuals are stuck in a frustrating meeting discussing for the third time some obscure point. They are not at all satisfied. They are not getting value from the meeting. Their project is late. They are, in fact, constantly frustrated. And half the attendees are from the supplier or vendor. Look around most cities and gaze through those glass windows – I'd estimate that about 50% of people feel they are wasting their time.

The Agile Manifesto calls us to sort out a few things:

1. Deliver. No compromise. No excuses.
2. Make valuable things.
3. Prioritize. (By implication, avoid distractions.)

I recently pressurized a multi-million dollar top-selling European B2B sales exec into telling me the shortest possible working week he could do and still hit his figures. He said two days.

We have to know who our customer is. Freelancers know this. They have to send an invoice. For those of us in companies, it can be less clear but no less important. Who pays the bill? If our work is internal, who is our customer? What is valuable to them? Let's prioritize that.

Instead of delivering valuable things, we could attempt the strategy of sucking-up to people. But in the end, whilst we may achieve our goal of staying safe, we just collude with a power structure of individuals each covering the arse of the other. Surely it's better to get stuff done?

What this level of focus requires, though, is some serious saying "no" skills. Saying "no" to pointless meetings, projects without a need, work that is less than inspiring. I trained for a while under a psychotherapist who often remarked, "Yes is no and no is yes." Saying "no" to one thing creates the space to say "yes" to another.

We are also delivering something earlier than expectations. I love saying to clients that, "We can make it faster than you can decide to do it and review it." I'm yet to be proved wrong. When designing a magazine or a short workshop, I can focus a team in a room, for a couple of days. With the right brief, this highly talented team of ten can get 20 days work done in two days, no sweat. Generally, our clients can't handle a review timeline of less than a couple of weeks. Only one client in the history of Interactive Workshops has expressed concern that we might be able to work so quickly.

So what might that mean to the average knowledge worker in a global-service business? Here are some tips:

1. Say "no" to everything possible that cannot be defined as a deliverable for a customer.
2. Decide on a spec and a reasonable amount of effort for anything we are working on. E.g. a ten-slide deck with 30 words per page.
3. Allocate to the task only the time we want to spend on it. In the case of the above, 45 minutes.
4. Use a correct sequence. For our example, a technically correct sequence would be:

   // Define the audience, focusing on a single member.
   // Define our main message in one sentence.
   // Sketch on a piece of paper the ten points for each slide in a ten-box storyboard.
   // Write the points in a document numbered one to ten in a consistent format, for example: heading, point.
   // Paste them into PowerPoint using the correct template.
   // Add graphics during the remaining time.
   // Check and add builds if there is time.

5. Set a tight deadline that is publicly committed to in calendars and to the client.
6. Repeatedly beat the deadline.

My old mentor Jim used the expression "conspiracy of non-delivery" for any situation where senior people spent months debating "strategy" without coming up with the goods.

When we work in our organization's office, we don't get out of bed, commute all that way, deal with the discomfort of hot desking, frazzle on the way home, to not get anything done. We came to deliver something valuable. To a client. As soon as possible. Let's do it!

Conspiracy of non-delivery: Any situation where senior people spend months debating "strategy".

CHANGE IT?
OF COURSE!

Agile Manifesto Rule #2: Welcome change requests, even late in projects. Agile processes harness change for the customer's competitive advantage.

"Welcome" is a brilliant word. It's positive, friendly, eager even. Welcoming change requests, even late in a project requires a crystal-clear mindset. A robust ego. And bags of empathy.

Welcoming change requests is the preserve of emotionally intelligent people: Those who are self-aware and in control of their thoughts, feelings and actions; those who can say, "Yes, sure", when their impulse is to be frustrated, upset or defensive. When we have worked hard, really hard, on something and then our client or boss says, "Actually, I want it this way", it's so tempting to be annoyed. Being annoyed is the easy choice. Being responsive is the difficult choice. Listening. Understanding. Remaining Zen.

How often do we get things perfect? Body? Partner? Finances? Diet? Holiday? Getting it perfect seems simple. Yet getting it perfect – especially first time – is an unlikely, if not impossible, goal.

Remember, agile is about delivering valuable things. Like diamonds, our job doesn't have to be flawless to achieve its aims. Change requirements are a way of our clients, bosses or colleagues saying, "This would be even more valuable if ..." They are actually helping us to do the best job we can, together. When we welcome change, we build something more valuable, which gives our clients a competitive advantage.

Plus we create deeper relationships. We signal, "Yes, you can ask me that, even late in a project. I'll always be listening. And I will always respond to that positively, if I humanly can." People who respond badly to change requests are whacking up a barrier and making it harder for the other person to ask again next time.

So welcoming change requests makes a better working product, improves our clients' competitive advantage and boosts our relational equity. Sounds like the optimum strategy.

There are alternatives. Another strategy is to not welcome change requests. Not to manage our emotions so others can contribute. To justify. Or Blame. In extremis, it's toxic. But even subtler, more passive-aggressive reactions can have a damaging effect on our relationships and the quality of our work.

Another strategy, for fear of having to adjust, is to spend days, weeks and months, planning, building coalitions, discussing or refining blueprints, but not really starting anything. Ensuring that every decision is made through a consensus, so that if it proves poor, or sub-optimal, responsibility is shared by an amorphous group of other executives. But is that really the life we want to live?

Radically simpler, is to welcome change requests, even late in the day. In Danny Wallace's excellent book, *The Yes Man*, he chooses to live an entire year saying "yes" to anything and everything. He chooses "yes" as his new moral code. Moral codes reduce decision-making. There's no need to think, if we are going to respond "yes" every time. No inner agony. No deliberation. No justification.

The US marines have a slogan: "Suck it up." Cyclists say, "We suffer in training, so we can suffer more in the race." Embracing change requests, even late in a project, with a stoic determination that, "This will make me better, the relationship better, the project better." Now that's what we are talking about.

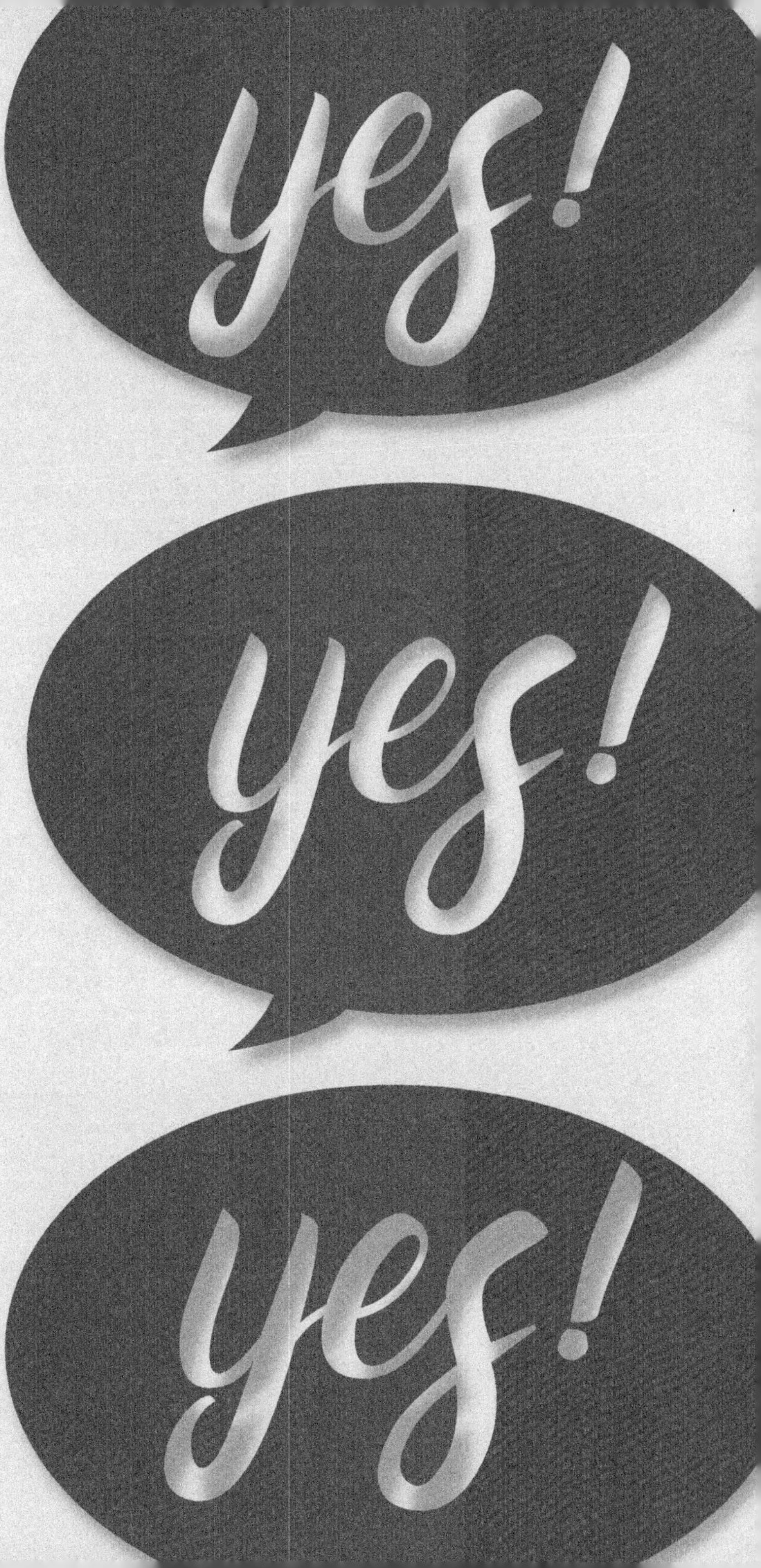
yes!
yes!
yes!

WE CAN MAKE IT. FAST

Agile Manifesto Rule #3: Deliver working products frequently, from a couple of weeks to a couple of months, with a preference for the shorter timescale.

Let's ask this: Who chooses to put themselves under extra time pressure? Very frequently in working life, we are asked to do something. The smart people out there ask for a deadline. The really smart people then impose their own, earlier deadline. It's a beautiful strategy. At its core is belief. "We can do what you need, faster than you need it."

Part of this strategy, as with all things agile, is choosing small-chunk milestones rather than big-chunk milestones. You could say small-chunk milestones are milestones, but big-chunk milestones become millstones.

I learned this lesson partly as a closing strategy and partly to help me overcome procrastination. Most of the time, clients give realistic project timelines. But working to a client deadline was a bit stressful. And some clients gave no deadline at all. They vaguely asked, "When do you think you can get it done by?"

Now, next month seems alluring. But next month has no urgency. My stock answer became, "The end of this week." Suddenly, writing a concept or a proposal had to be done now.

Or on the plane. Or on Thursday. Or early Friday morning.
But this week. Finished. Done. Sent.

And a little bit of psychology made me realise it couldn't be
sent at 8 pm on Friday. That makes me look, late, rushed, poor
at time management. I wanted to signal to clients that it was
well within my capability and I was in control. So the thing
needed to be in their inbox at 4 pm on Friday. The metagame
had begun.

One of the many benefits of sending something before the
week is out is that we prove we can deliver. Conversely, there
is something about waiting around for a few weeks that
seems to open up a whole world of complexity, ambiguity
and doubt.

Imagine you are selling a house and you have two buyers, one who will be ready to move within a month and the other who can't be ready for three months. There is something alluring about the fast-moving buyer. And a lot less that can go wrong.

Another benefit is that delivering small things frequently increases the connection and empathy between the worker and the client/boss. If I do something great for you every day, or every week, trust builds. The relationship grows.

Finally, we give our clients a better chance to review something properly. In a recent project our team created 45 different client assets, each of about a day's work. If you were the client, what would you rather receive?

1. A document a day for nine weeks?
2. Five documents on a Friday each week?
3. Or 45 documents at the end of the project?

Receiving all the documents at the end of the project is disastrous. Days of reviewing (or no review) followed by days of amendments and wrangling. Another month of finalizing. Even the admin burden is high.

So choose shorter timescales. Make life simpler. Give everyone that good feeling. Build relationships. Shorter timescales allow us to welcome change requests and optimise the next bit of work.

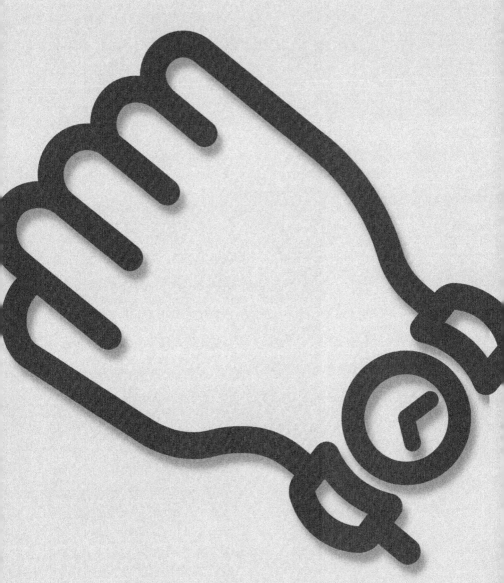

THE DAILY GRIND

Agile Manifesto Rule #4: Business people and developers must work together daily through the project.

Daily is strong. Daily is unequivocal. Working daily leaves us no room for escape.

In the digital world, working together can be ambiguous. Working together might be a WhatsApp, Skype, Slack and email-fueled virtual affair. Or it could be a hack-style, locked-in-a-room situation. Or it might be a daily meeting between the businessy types and developery types.

What's at the heart of this maxim?

// Don't work in isolation.
// Don't do our own thing, without daily input from those up and down the chain.
// Don't do things that don't make business sense.

When we're trying to satisfy our customers through the early and continuous delivery of valuable things, it's tempting to whack on our headphones, bunker down, switch off and block out reality. If we're involved in the creation of projects, it's also tempting to grow an ego about our own importance and understanding of it. But everyone's input is important, and "business people" are a necessity. Finance and control, marketing, purchasing. These people know what matters.

In one part of my career I had a job as a product manager. Every fortnight we had to go and demonstrate our latest product to the sales team. This was genuinely probably the most vomit-inducing part of any job I've ever had. (I've had two jobs that involved cleaning toilets – this was worse.) Why? Because business people will give very direct and honest feedback about what's wrong. Sometimes the whole thing was wrong. Suddenly, welcoming change requests isn't so easy, right?

BMW Group designed its innovation building in a honeycomb shape so that each team was no less than three meters from the three next most important teams. Finding a way to spend frequent time with decision makers, bosses and other important people who will help shape the commercial relevance of our work is a gamechanger.

Agile isn't really that hierarchical. We shouldn't be either. Imagine hiring a freelancer, but then not making ourselves available to shape decisions. Higher ups can and should be accessible. And if they are not, then it's down to us to get our influencing shoes on. My team is ace at this. They genuinely pin me down. They try to package their requests in a fun way. In return, I have to open up my diary.

If so called "business people" lack the availability to be involved in the daily grind of a key project, I would question their ability. As a good friend in ad-land told me a while ago, "It's no longer cool to be busy." This is from a man studying trends, demographics and culture. "Busyness is for shmucks," he implied.

We need to get control of our diaries. Get control of our priorities and make space for important, urgent things. Status seekers love a full diary. Outcome-focused delivery people make time to shape and work on important projects. And not just in the margins. Not just over lunch. Or out of hours. They will make quality space available in the meat of their working day.

THIS PROJECT NEEDS YOU

Agile Manifesto Rule #5: Build projects around motivated individuals. Give them the environment and support they need, and trust them to get the job done.

Emma Wiggs is one seriously motivated individual. I first met her at the National Watersports Center. The Paralympic-gold-medal-winning, world champion, world-record-holding athlete was speaking to a group of 30 execs between gym sessions and massage. She let rip for 45 minutes with the disarming honesty of someone who has thought life through deeply. This is a sportswoman who has dedicated every part of her life to achieving her goals. Giving up a career. Succeeding in two disciplines.

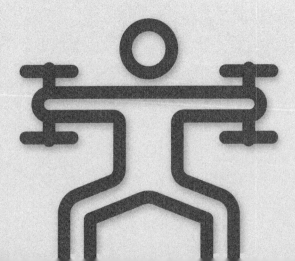

Steve is different. Calm, confident, discrete. Around a campfire with another 30 execs, he shares very simply how we all have the innate power to be the best we can be, if we can only dedicate ourselves to it. Steve shares what happens when we overdo it. He talks about stress and trauma. He is one of the UK's top coaches to people in high-stress jobs. Supporting police who deal with terrorism. Coaching brain surgeons in techniques that can help their fingers remain steady as they operate. Training senior executives in the world of finance making massive investment decisions.

The list goes on. Nathan is a machine that can tear down metaphorical walls at work. Emily is the bounciest, most energizing colleague. Simon is discrete, considered and on it every single day. Johnny is at his desk getting stuff done at 7:30 am when his flight back from Germany touched down at 10 pm the night before. Susan is controlled, on it, relaxed. Andy, for nearly nine years now, has been hitting country after country, rolling up his sleeves, keynoting for client after client and leading delivery teams.

Managing motivated people is easy. It's the winning difference. It's not about a pay raise, status, promotion, job grade. But an inner drive that fires up and says, "Right, let's do this." Selfless. Humble. But dripping with the powerful elixir of a can-do person. Martial valour. Warrior spirit.

Leadership theorists and self-help gurus often suggest finding our inner motivation. How do we do this? Looking within ourselves is important. Plugging into job roles we enjoy. Doing things we have a talent for. The Emmas, Steves and Nathans of this world have taken it to another level by aligning their internal and external motivations. Emma is supremely self-motivated. But the stimulus of another world title does no harm at all.

So build teams around motivated individuals. Or find people who can become motivated like them. And align those people with project roles they have a passion for and are good at.

Next up are the environment, support and trust.

Those people above. They don't need much. And, at the same time, they require a great deal. Motivated individuals don't compromise. They don't put up with issues over years. They don't work somewhere that's constantly a pain in the arse. They don't work for bosses who are slippery. They have an incisive urgency. Drive. So pull out all the stops and get them what they need. Or lose them.

The Gallup survey that charts employee engagement asks a telling question, "I have the materials and equipment I need to do my work right." On a practical level, do our teams have the resources they need to get the job done? Don't let a piece of equipment or software stand in the way of getting the job done quickly, easily and efficiently.

Do our teams have the support they need? Again, it doesn't always take much. A coffee at the right moment. Some meaningful encouragement. A bit of care. Lightening a difficult moment. Expanding their horizons. Suggesting interesting people to work alongside and learn from. Helping very committed and focused people prioritize home life and outside interests. Having them over for dinner.

Emma Wiggs has the motivation (a world title), the environment (a world-class gym and a purpose-built lake) and the support (friends, family, coaches, physios, psychologists). And boy does she get on with the job.

Motivated individuals can get the job ... DONE.

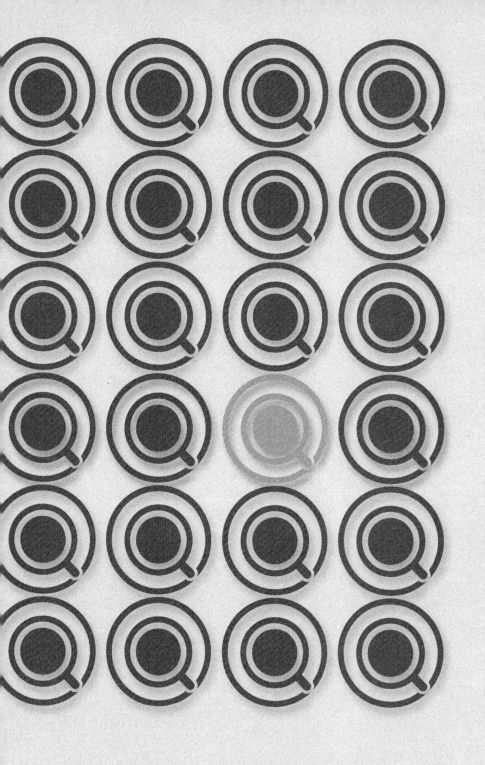

LET'S MEET

Agile Manifesto Rule #6: The most efficient method of conveying information to and within a team is face-to-face conversation.

Our freelance, super-tech, VUCA world needs more face time. For a number of years, I refused to communicate with my team through email. To start with I just asked them not to email me. When they persisted, I said I considered it a personal slur on our relationship and a breakdown in our communications if they emailed me. When that failed, I said emailing me would result in an HR disciplinary.

Why the resistance? Face-to-face communications are a high-context tool. What that means is there is lots of information happening in F2F comms. Not just the words. Moods, energy and trust are all mixing together with the verbal information.

When my dad had a motorcycle accident, I spoke for several days with my mum about his situation before I visited. And when I visited I was reminded again that – even with the greatest effort from both sides, by well-known individuals, with polished communication skills – the most effective method of conveying information within a relationship is face to face.

People are afraid of meetings, not because meetings themselves are wrong, but because the meetings we have are so ineffective. When we step into agile worlds, we are not just meeting. We are normally:

1. Making something.
2. Delivering something.
3. Receiving important feedback.
4. Involving key business people in a project.

Agile meetings have very a clear purpose. When done well, face-to-face meetings are an investment. When done badly, face-to-face meetings are a cost. Plain and simple.

Working together face-to-face promotes high-bandwidth troubleshooting and resolution. Our team meets briefly at 9:06 each morning for our first meeting of the day, "Office Awesome". We have one minute each to communicate our main priorities for the day ahead. There's no discussion. Those few minutes pay off over the remaining seven hours we work. The ROI is easy. Ten minutes, to improve 420 minutes. We gain clarity, motivation, momentum, deadlines and focus for 420 minutes, from just ten minutes. When I say to the group I will spend a maximum of one hour building a meeting agenda, somehow it becomes more real. The face-to-faceness of it is brilliant.

When we start spending time in meetings that are seriously productive, and help us get ahead of the curve of delivery, then we start prioritizing being in meetings.

A couple of years ago, a client asked us to create a product at very short notice. We had to build and implement a three-week assessed sales training for people from seven countries. We had two months to create it, get in country and launch it. We agreed to the project on two provisos. Firstly, that we did agile. Secondly, that we had the key meetings face-to-face.

A timeline was laid out that included:

1. A kick-off workshop in Switzerland of one day to agree the architecture of the programme.
2. A two-day troubleshooting workshop in Hong Kong to review and improve all the assets.
3. A one-day face-to-face workshop in Vietnam just ahead of the programme to finalize all the details and brief the team.

Urgency streamlined all the client decision-making. Face-to-face meetings allowed rapid, outcome-focused work; feedback all the whilst building trust, clarity and commitment.

The maths behind email comms is pretty bad. If I spend five minutes writing an email, and you spend five minutes reading it, and then five minutes thinking about how to reply, then five minutes replying, and then I read it for five minutes, think about it for five minutes and then reply for five minutes ... we are 30 minutes into our discussion. Next time you have a discussion, see how much can be achieved in a 30-minute timeframe. The conversation is about ten times more effective. "Ah!" The emailers say. "But email allows us to have a record of what was said!" Who are you? The FBI? HMRC? A solicitor? What kind of outfit are you in that needs quasi-legal records of what was said. And, to be blunt, you can always whack out a few bullet points whilst you talk.

Zoom meetings almost work. In the same way watching a movie on your phone almost has the same effect as the cinema. In theory, there's not much difference. But one is an experience with popcorn, buzz and a whole range of emotions. The other is just a trip on the tube.

One final point. What else are we going to do with our spare time? Adopting the level of productivity the Agile Manifesto creates, we will have a fair bit more capacity to go to meetings. Lets do it!

SHIPPING IS THE METRIC

Agile Manifesto Rule #7: Working products are the primary measure of progress.

Signed, sealed, delivered? Shipped. Done and dusted. Finished. Sent. Completed. Finito.

Shipping a working product feels great. That is the primary measure of progress. Finished. Maybe not perfect. But working. And sent.

Freelancers simply cannot invoice until their work is done. For salaried workers, imagine if our daily salary only got paid when we had completed all the work agreed for the day, nothing rolling over to tomorrow. Because that is what we are competing against. We are working in direct competition with a freelancer, who has no bonus, no guarantee, no performance review, but also no internal meetings, no other responsibilities and a laser focus that if they don't ship the work they committed to, they are out of a job. With the big change we are experiencing in the labour market, shareholders are being asked to decide which is more cost effective: Freelancers or perms? And freelancers are easier to manage. No need for career conversations. No employee-engagement survey. So, for those of us who are employed, let's ship that work. Freelancers are the competition. Workers must outperform them. We have to ship more than those outsource agents.

Inputs are a terrible metric. We can spend hours in meetings, months in planning, invest cash, time, effort and energy, all the while looking swish in a business shirt or skirt using some nice stationary to take notes. All the grand theories. All the meetings. But shipping work is the only metric.

What am I shipping? What am I getting done? Working products as frequently as possible. Embracing agile allows shipping not to just be the metric, but also to become the job.

To ship a product it has to be finished. I've had tens of people work for me over the years. I fall in love with those who turn up with their work finished. Those that turn up with it nearly finished are, frankly, a nightmare. You can't ship nearly finished work. You can't ship a document that still has one image missing. You can't ship a magazine with brilliant copy, but no front cover. You can't ship a presentation that hasn't been proofread. You can't ship an email that is missing a key date. You can't ship a workshop without an agenda. You can't ship a marketing event without all the collateral printed. You can't ship a consultant to another country without a flight and a passport. Details matter. Take responsibility. Take full responsibility. Bring it finished. So we can ship it.

Working on one thing at a time is vital. Imagine working on five products. If each is 95% finished, we can ship nothing. The same effort applied sequentially means four products are finished. So let's ship those. Now we can direct all our efforts on the final product and get it from 75% complete, to finished.

Two pieces of work to do? Ship one at lunchtime. Ship one at the end of the day. Don't work on both and try to ship them. Because that last-minute interruption at 4:30 pm? That means nothing gets shipped today.

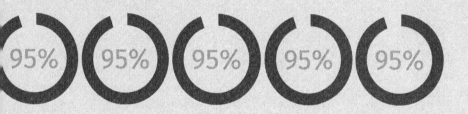

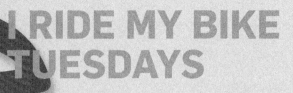

I RIDE MY BIKE TUESDAYS

Agile Manifesto Rule #8: Agile processes promote sustainable work rates. The sponsors, developers and users should be able to maintain a constant pace indefinitely.

Tuesday night's "chaingang" is epic. At a crossroads in West London, 20-odd cyclists arrive from 7:15–7:30 pm for a 90-minute blast down a highly specific route, "The Pearson Chaingang", a segment on Strava. Flying out of Richmond, right across the Thames, then left towards Hampton Wick, there's a 10k warm up before things get deadly serious. A Lycra-clad, carbon-armed cage fight, where youthful up-and-coming bikers from the London club scene pit their wits against balding middle-age city pros splashing the cash annually on a top-end bike.

Every Tuesday I have a little schoolboy tummyache: Nerves. At 5 pm it turns into an adrenaline-fuelled body tingle. I have a very light bite to eat. Get out of work. Gear on. Check the tyre pressure. Head to Sheen. Bella, Drew, Robin, Helen, Tom, Will, Al, Bruce and others are all heading to the same spot.

We are all there to answer one question. Can we maintain the pace? Chaingang is a "no wait" ride. If you are spat out the back, breathing hard, legs burning, face covered in snot, that's it. Some current and ex-pros will try to shatter the teamwork with repeated hard efforts. Sometimes there's the euphoria of staying in at the top of the final hill. Sometimes you find yourself riding through a dark London street, alone, watching the red lights of the group leave you.

Work can feel like this. Our bodies and minds – fatigued by effort, drained by deadlines, ruined by years of burning the candle at both ends – slowly give up. We gain weight, neglect our marriages, fail to pop in on our parents, reduce our circle of friends. Agile recognizes that urgency can be an everyday experience. But it doesn't have to end in a deficit. We need to find a constant pace that we can maintain indefinitely.

As a fan of reverse psychology, I see working late as a sign of weakness. Working late occasionally is natural. It says that, due to something unexpected, I'm putting in a shift to get this done. But it is not possible to work intensely, productively and fruitfully every day.

Working in an agile environment means there is always a short-term goal. Once we have achieved it, we are done for the day. Getting working products shipped by 4:30 pm means we can also have a life.

Tuesday nights are massive for me, personally. For 15 years I held no regular out-of-work commitments. A different country every week. A different continent every month. I wasn't working "late", but work disrupted the rhythm of my life. That's ok for a season. Agile's founders recognize that we can work for a period of time where we have to make compromises outside of work. But not forever.

Life must be lived at a tempo we can sustain indefinitely. And not just for us. For our stakeholders. Our board of directors. Our partner. Our friends.

So put the chaingang, or whatever you do, in the diary and keep it there. If nothing else, it helps us remember to leave work and do something we enjoy.

THINK LIKE JOBS, YEAH?

Agile Manifesto Rule #9: Continuous attention to technical excellence and good design enhances agility.

Who's the technical expert? Who's the good designer? Agile requires technical expertise. In order to achieve something valuable in a short timeframe, and then repeatedly deliver further valuable things indefinitely, we need to be good.

It's great working with a technical expert. What takes a normal person a few hours is done in minutes. What seems intractable is rapidly solved. What sounds like a new and complex problem, well, it's been solved before. Technical expertise is the bedrock of high performance.

Technical experts can also accurately estimate how long things are going to take. They can speak authoritatively to clients, customers and team members based on experience not knowledge, wisdom not ego. Technical experts can ignite a team because their technical strengths enable others to bring what they are good at. Yet in our own corner or cubicle, we can build our technical expertise. To start with, we can become tech-spert at the basic skills of business life:

// Running meetings.
// Running projects.
// Communicating and presenting.
// Motivating others.

Do you touch type? At the latest count I can do a fairly accurate 80 words per minute without looking at my keyboard. It's a level of expertise that has paid off repeatedly over my business career, enabling me to outperform peers in emailing, report writing and presentation making.

Deep knowledge of our field can be accumulated rapidly with an inquisitive, open mind and the company of the right people. Someone once said, "You can't outperform your inner circle." We can ask ourselves, "Does my inner circle contain people much, much better than me?" If so, we will raise our game.

Combine technical expertise with good design. Good design is not just what looks good. It also needs to perform, convert, astonish and fulfil its purpose. Now we are talking. The maverick innovators like Jobs, Dyson and Musk all combined technical expertise with good design to produce industry-redefining products.

Prototyping, storyboarding and sketching are all ways of creating initial working designs. Car companies build prototypes out of clay. Architects make blueprints and scale models. Movie directors draw storyboards. Working to a great blueprint is a gamechanger.

Watch how people create a PowerPoint presentation. Very often they just sit down and start. The Interactive Workshops crew always start with a sketch. They spend five minutes on paper making a rough version, making sure they are paying attention to good design. Simple, but with sufficient flourish to capture the imagination. Something technically swish that others would find hard to replicate. Something that works as a tool for its intended purpose. Elegant, beautiful, effective.

Technical experts with design flair use two important aspects of the psyche. The technical part utilizes our process-oriented, detail-focused rational brain. The design flair utilizes our big-picture, creative and conceptual imagination. Not everyone can master both skillsets. However, in agile, being good at one is not enough.

TOO LAZY TO CLOCK ON

Agile Manifesto Rule #10: Simplicity – the art of maximizing the amount of work not done – is essential.

Johnny and I both agree we are lazy. A special kind of lazy. We are too lazy to clock-on to a bad job. We love working hard. We are happy to work really hard. But clocking-on to a duff job – frustrating, hard to finish, over-complex, not well managed – we're not interested and too lazy to sign-up to that.

Johnny and I believe deeply in maximizing the amount of work not done. Work life is full of noble, virtuous and dedicated individuals driven to deliver to a high standard, come what may. This attitude is to be respected, and no doubt achieves a great deal. Yet it suffers from the same high-compound interest effect that makes a payday loan a terrible idea.

In essence, the most noble are often pedaling a perfectionist scam that, when analyzed in detail, is an incredible waste of time in every single department, involving tens of like-minded people. We could call it a Ponzi scheme of ineffective waste.

Let's use the example of a presentation, because a great number of people spend their life making presentations. Imagine a presentation for an hour. Our valiant and noble worker decides 40 slides will do it. Comprehensive. Good. Solid. They work for ten minutes per slide. That's 400 minutes (just shy of seven hours) work. These 40 slides are sent to a colleague for a proofread. Another 120 minutes. Then a graphic designer works on them for a day because it's a key client proposal. Another 450 minutes. We are over a thousand minutes in. But we are not finished ...

There's a snag with the key messaging. The flow is adjusted, but the key message links on all the slides need reworking. Feedback from the boss is incorporated. Back to graphics. Back to the proofreader. Then we rehearse. It's quite quickly apparent that we can only properly get through one slide every three minutes. The presentation has to be slimmed down to 15 slides. But we can't just delete 25 slides. No. All the slides need reworking into a new narrative. The 45 slides are printed out. The key models are good, but won't fit onto one slide. Everything is edited down again. Still no good. At this point, the real narrative emerges and we get a clear flow for 15 simple slides. There is very limited text. A few key graphs.

We arrive to present. They are running 20 minutes late. We have 40 minutes. The audience is broadly positive. At slide six the senior client says, "Great, we get it. Can we talk costs?" We skip to side 14. They approve. We have created nearly 2,000 minutes of work when we could have done it in 90. This pattern of time fraud happens in every organization.

Maximizing the amount of work not done is an art. Simplicity is saying, "Let's do something small, aesthetically beautiful, that serves its purpose." Keeping specifications light. Keeping meetings short. Keeping involvement to a minimum. Inviting two people to a meeting rather than six. Knowing how to say "no" tactfully or firmly to the kind offer of certain responsibilities. Avoiding, with great skill, anything that sounds like a cross-functional working group. Using boundaries and guile to keep out of situations that sound time intensive and outcome poor. At times it's a dark art. But simplicity, the art of maximizing the amount of work not done, is essential.

SORT IT YOURSELF

Agile Manifesto Rule #11: The best architectures, requirements and designs emerge from self-organizing teams.

Affordances are clues about how an object should be used, typically provided by the object itself or its context. For example, even if you've never seen a coffee mug before, its use is fairly natural. The handle is shaped for easy grasping and the vessel has a large opening at the top with an empty well inside.

In the same way that we don't really need an instruction manual for a coffee cup, so a half decent group of individuals can work out how to get their work done as a team.

Before the industrial revolution those peasant farmers didn't require a boss for their scrap of land. The blacksmith had no board of investors for his shop. For about 150 years we have chosen to work in systems that have a foreman, supervisor, leader or boss. Yet the best teams don't need that.

But wait. It's a smidge more complicated than that. Because some people in teams want a boss. Over many years of corporate team buildings I have repeatedly witnessed leadership actively reducing group function. Time and again, leader-led teams have failed where self-organizing teams have succeeded. For those of us working in teams, here is a dare. Take the initiative. Take as much initiative as possible. Be brave. Be bold. Work together. Get the job done brilliantly. Agile reinforces that the best work is done by self-organizing teams. Self-organizing teams develop patterns, dialogues, routines and methods to get the job done as effortlessly as possible. Throw in a "captain" and we also introduce a pinch point, someone who needs to be pleased, someone with a bit too much pressure to direct. Someone whom we might just obey rather than challenge.

We can easily point the finger at the leaders. Yet it's a two-way street. If we, as team members, can demonstrate the initiative and deliver working products, seek feedback, run reviews, keep things simple, then there is no need for a boss to do that for us. In corporate structures we will need to wrap all this up with some pretty solid communication to our boss (whom we could think of as a sponsor). When we are working in dysfunctional or under-skilled teams then it is likely that a superior with more experience and some power to bring clarity will help. But the best teams don't need that. A goal then shapes up nicely. How quickly can we not need our boss? How quickly can we build our strength as a unit so we don't need a leader? Many organizations have a highly autonomous culture with excellent people, and great processes that mean leadership can be light and supportive rather than heavy and directive.

Self-organizing teams also build a sense of collective responsibility. This builds the security of individual members and gives a sense of belonging, greater than the bosses approval. Human beings are social animals. At times we have the same herd instincts as sheep. Yet with the same understanding of who is top dog as wolves. Running with the pack is great fun.

Freelancers have worked out how to thrive unmanaged. So why can't those of us in organizations take courage from their confidence and figure out a way to get things shipped without hierarchical oversight. Turns out ... we can!

EVEN BETTER IF

Agile Manifesto Rule #12: At regular intervals, the team reflects on how to become more effective, then tunes and adjusts its behaviour accordingly.

Dad always said, "The biggest room in the world is the room for improvement."

Whilst working at BAE Systems I was in awe of our client's meeting process: Without fail, every meeting ended at 55 minutes past the hour. The final five minutes were dedicated to flip-charting 1) "what went well" and 2) what could be improved ("even better if..."), with contributions required from all team members at all levels.

During a recent marketing hack, we assembled at the start of day two to review our Kanban board. Removing all the "shipped" items from day one, we reprioritized the issues left to complete. We shared a piece of growth-mindset feedback for each individual. We worked our way round. It turned out that I needed to be more available. In attempting to hit the deliverables, I had left team members stranded. In private afterwards, a key senior freelancer, Emmie (west London's most-loved marketing consultant) said, "Wow. That daily feedback must really mitigate the need for tough conversations. I mean, if you get improvement feedback all the time, I can't imagine you have any really big issues."

It's true. Creating a high-frequency growth-mindset feedback culture means nothing mounts up. Problems are aired. Issues addressed. Today. Now. It's not personal. "Can you please do more of x, y and z, and just a bit less of a, b or c?" Sure. No sweat.

"How can I improve?" Four simple words. Quick and easy to ask co-workers, clients, bosses, family, friends. It says, "My door is open and my defences are down."

Tuning and adjusting builds behavioural flexibility in all workers, reducing the emotional burden of bringing up tricky issues. Tuning and adjusting behaviour is a pleasure.

High-frequency growth-mindset feedback cultures also love to periodically sit back and reflect on how they can improve. "Continuous improvement" sounds dated now. So maybe use the Japanese kaizen "Change for the better", if you need to sound cool.

When teams powerfully engage with improvement culture in a non-critical way, they start to motor. Sometimes with extraordinary results. To do this takes a bit of grit. The hardest part of what BAE systems did was not the conversation. It was the discipline to finish the meeting by 55 minutes past the hour. Think about that.

CHAPTER 3

THE AGILE LEADERSHIP MANIFESTO

LEADING TEAMS THAT GET IT DONE

Agile Manifesto Rule #1: Our highest priority is to satisfy the customer through early and continuous delivery of valuable "things".

Really, leading teams is simple. Plan the work. Work the plan. We could leave it there. When we put all the agile principles together – short deadlines; clear metrics; the right, effective meetings; good design; technical experts; self-organizing, client-responsive, well-balanced people who ask for feedback – so we plan the work. And then we work the plan.

So, what's the role of the leader? Many people would say vision. But, taking that metaphor a bit further, I'd say the leader's job is focus. Focusing the energy, effort, momentum, excitement and energy, and getting the work, not started, but done.

Working in sprints helps. Having a feedback culture helps. But most organizations start off on a difficult footing by using a hierarchy and then individualizing every job role so that no teamwork is required.

Team-theory gurus Katzenbach and Smith define a team as:

"A small group of people with complementary skills who are committed to a common purpose, performance goals and approach for which they are mutually accountable."

Their seminal team study identifies that most of us who work in teams are actually in a working group. But if we can make teams, then we can realise enormous performance gains.

In the creative industries, teams can range from a team of two – a creative partnership – to enormous account teams. That unit of two is a fascinating case study. Accountability, complementary strengths, someone to have lunch with. At a minimum, a team of two allows a few different ways to get the job done.

True teams have an 'esprit de corps' that allows them to commit and get the job done. Ultimately, the aim is that these teams become self-organizing, with a culture and modus operandi of their own, deeply imbedded, unconscious, instinctive. True teams can be left to get on with it. Great leaders can run several of these teams.

So, what's the leader's job now? In organizations, it's mainly removing barriers. Breaking down Chinese walls. Moving difficult people on. Streamlining. Removing personal bad habits. Deleting over-complex processes. Making life as simple as possible.

Teams do need vision. But they mostly need a sense of achievement, progress and satisfaction. They thrive with self-generated goals, ownership. So they need team leads or senior people that release them to get on with it. Leaders that communicate ceaselessly about the value of shipping work. Of satisfying the customer by providing them repeatedly with valuable things.

And they need a leader who has their back. More than providing vision or focus, they want a boss who provides security and support. Who is an anchor. A rock. Top leadership guru and former hostage negotiator George Kohlrieser calls this strategy "Care to dare". We can unleash astonishing potential in teams if we can be their secure base when it all goes wrong.

As we will see...

CREATING CULTURES THAT SAY: "CHANGE IT? OF COURSE!"

**Agile Manifesto Rule #2:
Welcome change requests, even
late in projects. Agile processes
harness change for the customer's
competitive advantage.**

Very simply, we create teams that can respond to customer change positively when we ourselves are responsive to our team. The best leaders enable and actively encourage colleagues to explore and take risks. How? By building trust.

Adults and children need security in their relationships. It's a basic human need. Without security we feel somehow lost in the world and unsafe. From a young age we orientate ourselves around our primary-care givers – normally parents – and form an incredibly close bond or attachment that affects everything in childhood, including stress levels, confidence, physical and mental health.

As children, this bond is strengthened by our daily lives. With a "full cup" of confidence children are able to go off and explore, especially if encouraged by their parents. During these explorations they use up their security energy, and at some point become somewhat overwhelmed. They then look around

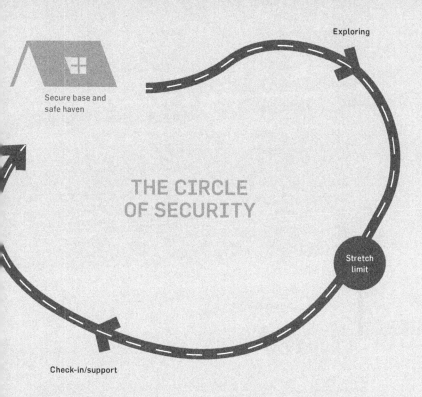

Exploring

Secure base and
safe haven

THE CIRCLE
OF SECURITY

Stretch
limit

Check-in/support

(when babies) or move/call etc. as they get older, to seek the
support of the primary-care givers, or of those to whom they
are attached. If they can't find a primary-attachment figure,
they may move to a secondary-attachment figure, such as
grandparents, teachers, etc.

We can represent this cycle of exploration and return with a
circle. In our adult life we still need attachment bonds. This
tends to be with our friends (in early adulthood) or partner/
spouse. The best leaders create this security for team
members. They enable and actively encourage colleagues
to go off and explore/take risks (empowerment) but, when
needed, are there for the team members to seek support.
If leaders are unable to implement the appropriate strategy
at the right time, the colleague starts to have feelings of
insecurity in the relationship and doesn't feel safe. The more
safe they feel, the more likely they are to take risks, step up to
greater responsibility and confidently fulfil their role.

Proximity

Definition: Proximity is about availability. One of a leader's priorities is to somehow be available for team members at the point of need. This could be on the end of a phone or via email. Attachment figures need to "be around" and to notice where their team members are on the circle and proactively encourage/support.

Example: The manager who makes a point of walking through the office every morning to say "good morning" and stops to have a focused conversation with at least one team member to find out how they are – even if it's only for a couple of minutes. This helps the manager to remain visible and approachable.

Question: What are you already doing that demonstrates you are available to others?

Openness

Definition: Encouraging another to express their thoughts and feelings. Leaders' skills in listening, empathy and handling emotion will allow team members to speak up about genuine thoughts, feelings or needs. Here we are aiming to listen to what support or encouragement might be required.

Example: The manager who listens when a team member confides in them about something small but personal is more likely to be approached about bigger or more troubling issues that may cause division in the relationship.

Question: Think of a time you shared something quite small but significant with someone and they really listened. How did that make you feel?

Responsiveness

Definition: Demonstrating empathy and action as a result
of an expressed need. When the leader is asked for help/
support/encouragement/a change of behaviour (e.g. you are
too controlling), they have a responsibility to action this.
If we hear, but don't respond, our relationship is weakened.
When we repeatedly listen and then respond, our relationship
is strengthened. As a result, individuals can take on more
responsibility, take more risks and stretch themselves.

Example: The manager who is asked for advice on time
management offers to meet the team member once a week
to coach them.

Question: What one thing could you do tomorrow to be more
responsive with your colleagues in your team?

When we do this with our teams, it is incredibly simple to
ask them to secure-base their clients. To take steps to be
proximate. To take steps to be open. To take steps to be
responsive. These three behaviours are the foundation of
success in any human relationship. Period.

FOCUSING A TEAM TO MAKE IT. FAST

Agile Manifesto Rule #3:
Deliver working products frequently,
from a couple of weeks to a couple
of months, with a preference
for the shorter timescale.

By now the message is clear: For an organization to succeed it must ultimately be able to deliver value faster than its client needs it. Accounts must get the month end done before the board meeting. Security must get the fans screened before the game. Doctors must get the patients diagnosed before they get really sick.

In physics, inertia and friction are the words that describe forces that hold us back. A key role for teams is to overcome both of these systematically.

Inertia

Much of the agile process – sprints, deliverables, face-to-face – is designed to provide clarity and overcome hesitation. It takes confidence to say, "We are not completely certain, but let's go for it." Cutting down decision-making time enhances effectiveness. Focusing on getting things done, rather than perfect, helps overcome the hesitation, "Are we setting out on the right path?"

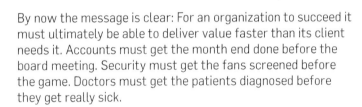

In physics, the bigger something is, the greater its inertia. Big things are hard to get rolling – in business as in life. Agile helps by breaking big things into little things. Yet still, big things are hard to get rolling.

Confidence plays a big part. Go-get-it, extrovert, charismatic leaders are looking for the next big thing. They want to kick off new initiatives. But that's not the only effective leadership style, by any means. If confidence can be unleashed across the team and this confidence can be harnessed, then confidence is multiplied. Confidence as a word has its roots in the Latin

cōnfīdō from con- ("with") + fīdō ("trust")

Overcoming inertia takes a leap of faith.

A few years ago our business had an impasse with the materials we created. They felt dry. We wanted to reboot. Do something creative. At an idea's meeting our most junior team member, Zoë, suggested a magazine format. This would take a great deal of effort, investment and, most importantly, we didn't know if we could do it. Whilst all confident people, it was a leap of faith. We gave ourselves one week to do it. Articles, contributors, edits, graphics, covers, photography. The whole works. Focusing a team really is that easy. A short deadline. A clear goal. The right kind of people. We locked ourselves in the upstairs room of a pub in Ealing. Sat down. And wrote.

Friction

Organizational friction is a different beast. This is the force that makes things harder work than they should be. People. Equipment. Processes. Rules. Focusing a team that can beat a client deadline means consistently "taking the stones from the shoes". A culture of small, continuous improvements helps. So does a positive attitude. If all team members ask often, "How can I improve?" then, step-by-step, friction is reduced.

Over longer time periods, people get more settled in the norm.

Working in teams over several years we accumulate debris in the system. So, from time to time, teams require a reboot. New blood. Some hiring or firing. A small re-org. Working a new system provides the opportunity to declutter. Having wandered into hundreds of organizations and worked with thousands of executives, I find it easy to spot a team that has become full of friction. Grinding to a halt. Great leadership creates a rapid, friction-free environment where all players contribute to improving the whole.

A culture of small, continuous improvements helps. So does a positive attitude.

THE AGILE LEADERSHIP MANIFESTO

REIGNITING JOY IN THE DAILY GRIND

Agile Manifesto Rule #4: Business people and developers must work together daily through the project.

Consistently working together daily requires mastery of the paradox of *structure* and the *spontaneous*.

Rhythms, patterns, processes, fixed agendas can all make the daily grind a joy. When they work well, smooth out life, provide reference points, make easy deadlines. Agile's sprint methodology gives any given day purpose. The short delivery schedules give focus, urgency. But sometimes that's not enough. Creating great teams also requires mastery of the spontaneous. To quote every football pundit, ever: "When to give them a kick up the bum and when to put an arm round them." Except both would now get you involved in a lawsuit. So please do neither.

Structure is well written about. The spontaneous is more of a secret. Any good story requires strong characters, a problem, a resolution and incidental detail. Joy can be ignited in the daily grind through creating these unpredictable, unstable elements. Which means our teams can come to work mostly clear that, "I know what will happen today", but with a part of them also thinking, " I wonder what is going to happen today." That is intrigue. That's why we go to movies, buy books, ask people out on dates. Not because we know exactly what will happen. But because we don't.

Work can be full of intrigue. Sales is full of intrigue. Meetings can be full of intrigue. Ad-land has a strategy of communication called "hide and reveal". This involves explaining, at length, the thinking behind the work. Then showing the work. It's a method of building suspense.

What's not to love about coming into a team where the processes and structures are brilliant and relatively frictionless, and there are positive, exciting twists and turns along the way. Being in the story, rather than merely observing it. Many people's work story is much more *Groundhog Day* than *Fifty Shades of Grey*. Not everyone wants a thrill. But a good team has excitement and unpredictability built in.

The spontaneity serves another purpose. It prepares us to respond to events. It is practice. Many organizations are so locked into their diaries, schedules and plans that there is very limited flex. Diaries are full for weeks in advance. Focusing on agility means saving space for everyone and encouraging effectiveness over busyness. Building the flex muscle in teams is a valuable part of an effective culture.

I'm always keen to ask team members, "What do your family and friends make of your job?" I often ask workshop participants, "What conversation are you having in your head on the train home?" When answered openly, this thinking gives a barometer reading of the current work situation. Narrative is key.

Agile requires that the team and business people work together daily. In doing so we build solid relationships focused around shipping working products. We work together to make the most effective work structures, and the most responsive team.

MOTIVATING TEAMS FULL OF GREAT PEOPLE

Agile Manifesto Rule #5: Build projects around motivated individuals. Give them the environment and support they need, and trust them to get the job done.

In many organizations, it is taken as fact that the people won't be great, so leaders of teams should accept average. This mindset is so persistent, so endemic, but so twisted; and yet, for many people, it is their daily norm.

I first encountered a radically different approach during my time as a graduate trainee at BMW Group. One day, Kev, my former manager, phoned me at 7:15 am. "Just phoning to find out when you are going to come and join me in the motorcycles division?" he said. I didn't really understand, but I was being headhunted. It turned out that the business wanted to grow its motorcycles business significantly and had appointed a radical new head of division. He had negotiated that he could achieve the goals, but only with his own hand-picked team. As a result, about seven people were exited from the team of 14. And in their wake a handful of go-get-'em, energizing new recruits were being brought in. I was 22 years old with neither motorcycle nor marketing knowledge. But Kev wanted me simply because of my attitude.

His management approach was simple. There were two of us. All jobs would be shared out regardless of status. Then we would get on and smash it. Kev knew how to run agile long before the concept was even formed. An opportunistic and tactical guy rather than a strategist. He believed in me. I was hooked. I was in. That year we raised our sales by 50%.

Leadership is about knowing how to assemble a team of great, motivated people, at least attitudinally, who want to kick on to the highest levels.

Paradoxically, motivating great teams is partially about eradicating poor performance and individuals without the right attitude. These are not easy decisions. And often they are marginal decisions. An average leader can make the obvious tough calls. A brilliant leader gets the marginal decisions right. When we as leaders duck these marginal decisions, the motivation of the whole team suffers, as does our leadership reputation.

A leader who consistently makes great marginal decisions creates a great deal of confidence. Crowd-sourcing input and opinion is vital in making marginal calls. So great leaders create an all-play environment around marginal decisions, sharing the intellectual, emotional and commercial challenge with the team. None of this is easy. Repeat. This is not easy. Moving on good people who are not quite good enough, or great people whose attitude sucks is very challenging. But it pays off. There is an important tangential benefit. Everybody knows poor attitude or underperformance will be handled directly and promptly. So they know it's down to them to keep up standards, culture, energy. They bring their A-game.

Working in a group of individuals who bring their A-game every day is intoxicating. England cricket captain Alistair Cook is one such player. Periodically, the England team would have a fitness test. Passing this test was required to be on the team. Alistair's approach was therefore to win every single element of every single training session. During his England career he was never beaten at a bleep test. He is the world record holder, having played 159 consecutive tests. And the highest scoring opening batsman of all time.

LEARNING TO MAXIMIZE GROUP TIME: LET'S MEET, BRIEFLY

Agile Manifesto Rule #6: The most efficient method of conveying information to and within a team is face-to-face conversation.

An observation over many years of consulting is that our organizational meeting cultures broadly suck. Static, turgid, dry, long, ineffective, oversubscribed, undersubscribed, too fluid, too structured, repetitive. For some reason, when people get together, it can be hard to find the bullseye. The bullseye is easily defined by three variables:

// Right content
// Right process
// Right dynamic

I recently sat through our weekly half-hour sales meeting, which I myself was running, thinking, "Wrong content, wrong process, wrong dynamic."

Ineffective face time is depressing. But worse, for some reason, we do it again and again. An ancient proverb I love says: "As a dog returns to its vomit, so a fool returns to their folly." Despite the massive frustration with some meetings, we keep going.

During an earlier phase of my career, I felt honoured to be invited on to a committee in the motorcycle industry. Until I found it was a full day a month, in Coventry, with some really dull people. Eventually, I realized I could take my to-do list and use the meeting to get some proper work done. Because I had no idea how to make it more effective.

Our most recent sales meeting was different. It was fully planned. This is what we achieved in 30 minutes:

2 minutes	Informal welcome ("How was your weekend?"), with pastries. Appointed a timekeeper.
2 minutes	Energizer from one of the team.
3 minutes	Quiz. Six facts about our year/month on a flipchart covered with Post-its. Each person had to guess one fact. Feedback given if they got it wrong and should have known better.
15 minutes	Five team members talked through a poster with their key monthly information on it.
1 minute	Talking through two key live-data sets from pre-tabbed web pages.
5 minutes	Personal action planning on the 30 open projects in our system.
1 minute	Discussing in pairs how to have the most effective week.
1 minute	Providing a score out of ten on the meeting effectiveness using a pre-printed card.

And we all left buzzing. Everybody contributed at least three times. Everybody stood up at least once. Of course, you can't keep this up for a day. But for our meeting, it was perfect.

When it comes to maximizing group time it is important to carefully think about the best processes. Processes affect the people dynamic. Human beings are highly sensitive to group effects and constantly, often without realizing, evaluate what is appropriate behaviour.

In our meeting, we used eight different meeting processes.

1. We started with the human touch for relaxation and to demonstrate empathy.
2. We had the energizer to get the blood flowing.
3. The quiz was to fire us up.
4. I provided the feedback to signal the need for accuracy in sales and financial matters.
5. The pre-printed posters were a prop so that individuals could stand up and present their key facts. Movement energizes people, gains commitment from the presenter and makes things real.
6. The planning phase allowed us to focus and ensure we all had our actions clear.
7. The paired discussion was to remind everyone of the support available from the team and to feel any challenges were listened to.
8. And the evaluation was so I could know if it had worked, and improve where needed.

Try this: Take one meeting next week. Sit down. Work out how to run it so it is brilliant, vibrant, hilarious, focused ... or whatever it should be.

Find the bullseye.

Keep working towards it.

SHIPPING IS THE METRIC. WHEN CAN WE SHIP THIS?

Agile Manifesto Rule #7: Working products are the primary measure of progress.

Agile culture loves shipping. So agile leadership requires all team members to ask, "When can we ship this?"
One school holiday, I had a job that involved actually shipping things. At 2 pm every day the night-freight lorry came. If the parcels were not ready, we let our customers down. Some days they were almost ready and I begged the driver for another five minutes. Yet if the van is late to the depot, nothing gets shipped.

Teams love deadlines. They love top-down deadlines. They love clear deadlines. They love early deadlines. But only when they are encouraged to work simply. When complex things are broken down into manageable chunks. Our shipping dialogues at Interactive Workshops go something like this:

Have we got a spec?

Yes

So how long do you think it will take?

Two hours

Great. So can we ship it in two hours?

Ummmm... Can you check it first?

Will I need to check it?

Ummm... no

Great! So when can we ship it?

In two hours

Team members here know exactly how much effort to put into the thing. They have no weeks of worrying. No working without being sure if they are on the right track. No stressing about whether they can make the deadline. They also know that if they do something else, they will struggle. So it provides total clarity on what to work on. No juggling. No multi-tasking. The work feels important. Clear and manageable. And, of course, whilst experienced and senior people don't need managing on an hourly basis, the truth is we all respond positively to this kind of clarity.

As project sizes grow, it's tempting to lay out a longer framework for the team. There is pressure to switch to a more "waterfall" approach. But self-organizing teams that get agile prefer a short deadline for smaller working or finished products. It is important that leadership keeps in mind the drive that comes from short deadlines. It actually relieves pressure on the team because it reduces uncertainty.

Consider a trip to the airport. The longer the trip, the more contingency is required. I live 15 minutes drive or 35 minutes tube ride from the airport. My journey planning is simple. If the traffic is bad, take the tube. If the tube is down, take a car! So easy. For many years, my sister lived 150 miles from the airport: One two-hour train, one interchange, another 20-minute train. But so much could go wrong it required a great deal of contingency. Very short deadlines for very small amounts of work make all our lives happy.

A good aim for a leader is for every team member to be able to get all their work done and get away on time, every single day. Late working is another form of contingency. If multiple team members are working late frequently, it is extremely likely there is a leadership issue.

EMBRACING PEOPLE WHO SAY: "I RIDE MY BIKE TUESDAYS"

Agile Manifesto Rule #8: Agile processes promote sustainable work rates. The sponsors, developers and users should be able to maintain a constant pace indefinitely.

Boundaries are good. Mostly. Agile culture is intense, no questions asked. The founders of agile clearly recognized the pace of life must be sustainable. Despite every project feeling important, agile helps teams because rather than one big looming deadline, there are lots of mini deadlines and lots of work delivered.

Great teams recognize the value of each member having a great social life, hobbies and family time. Great teams recognize that whilst getting the job done is vital, the way to do that is through effective use of work time, rather than prolonged, isolated hard work.

People who ride bikes on Tuesdays, have a dance class booked, have football training on Wednesday, have a church or family commitment, can't fly on Sunday because they promised ... These people are teaching us all something vital. They hold up a mirror that reminds us all to evaluate our priorities and know when and how to say, "no", "no thanks" or "not this time".

Leaders who become consumed by the work mission may well get a great deal out of their teams. But at what cost? Leaders who embrace commitment to the team, by definition value commitment. So we must respect their commitment when it is directed elsewhere.

What should not be tolerated is poor estimating, poor planning or poor execution. Individuals or teams that can't get it done are a problem. Their passion for fishing, salsa or travel is not.

Without people of passion, creativity and joy, how can our team really thrive? How can we arrive at work fresh? How can we train those who work with us not to ask us to do some vital work at 5:30 pm, but to plan better? How can we ensure delegation is methodical, fair, clear and early?

As mentioned earlier, I once got a verbal warning from my boss for going to a wedding. I had been asked to provide a set of product-evaluation figures by close of play on Friday. I spent several hours doing this, working diligently to get everything done for the 4 pm meeting. At 4 pm it turned out that my colleague, Debbie, had also been asked to pull some figures together, so we both came to the meeting with the data but in very different formats. Our CEO had failed to be specific. He hadn't asked us to work together or signalled that we were both working on data. At 5 pm on Friday, that didn't seem to matter to him. Very simply, I was told to re-do the whole piece of work by 8 am on Monday. I explained that at 6 pm I was taking a train to Scotland and would be at a wedding all weekend. In a few short sentences, I said that unfortunately I was unable to do five or six hours work as I was committed to spending that time with my wife. I explained that on other weekends it would be no problem. I also signalled that had the briefing been specific about format I could easily have done the work right first time, and would be happy to rectify it on Monday.

By Monday afternoon, my somewhat misguided boss, who I actually really liked, attempted to give me a verbal warning for lack of respect and being unreasonable. To be honest, I quite enjoyed his shocked face when I immediately tendered my resignation. "Don't you want to think about it?" he asked. "In fact, I think you should. I can't accept this. Take the rest of the day off and let's talk again tomorrow." "I'll happily take the rest of the afternoon off," I said. "And you'll have my resignation in writing first thing tomorrow morning."

Respecting boundaries is a prerequisite for trust. Trust is the foundation of teamwork. Of belonging. Of feeling safe. Great leaders 100% embrace people who say, "I ride my bike Tuesdays."

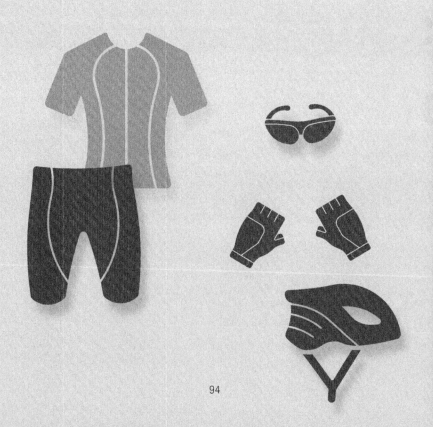

Respecting boundaries is a prerequisite for trust. Trust is the foundation of teamwork.

LEADERSHIP AND DESIGN THINKING SO YOU CAN "THINK LIKE JOBS, YEAH?"

Agile Manifesto Rule #9: Continuous attention to technical excellence and good design enhances agility.

How can leadership enhance technical excellence and good design? How can we encourage a continuous focus on those things? Two types of investment are required. The first is an investment in the training, growth and learning of individuals and teams. The second is a commitment by the leader to giving specific, detailed – and potentially unpopular – feedback.

Acquiring technical excellence takes practice, training and experience. My friend Pete is a very gifted musician. When his fingers hit the ivories and he starts to sing it is a wonderful thing. Often, he is not doing that much. A few chords. A simple melody. His excellence allows him to achieve a great deal very simply. Matteo is a great graphic designer. He has studied for many years. His layouts are magic. Karen is a powerhouse and ninja in growing businesses. Ninety minutes of Karen's simple advice can result in tens, even hundreds of thousands of pounds of business revenue. Karen, Matteo and Pete have invested in technical excellence. In doing so, they have worked out how to achieve great results very simply.

What a gift! Leaders of teams should pursue and develop such individuals if we are to benefit from the awesome productivity of an agile team.

They say, "A camel is a horse designed by committee." Great leaders allow technical experts to lead design work on a project, knowing that the vision of one great person is preferable to the compromise that is cobbled together from the wish list of a wide variety of uncommitted "stakeholders". The term, "intelligent design" has been hijacked by religious fundamentalists. Intelligent design in its purest sense makes every job from there on in easier.

Technical excellence and good design are also achieved by robust reviews and specific feedback. When working with leaders or facilitators on a training programme, I love helping them with the nitty gritty of the detail. Ditto, when designing a programme. It's a great joy to provide sophisticated improvement points. True mastery and great design comes iteratively. It comes by day-to-day working on small details. Great team leaders will make and take the time to do this; patiently, carefully, specifically.

Sometimes, for leaders, this is tough. It means providing cutting feedback in a sensitive way. It means screwing up plans and filing them in the trash. It requires iteration. Patience. Often it requires sleeping on things and coming back fresh in the morning. It can require retreat from blind alleys when much has been invested.

But isn't saying, "We've got it wrong", part of what leadership is? Isn't speaking truth to power, making unpopular decisions, insisting on the highest standard of quality – isn't that what leadership is?

Steve Jobs was apparently "difficult to work for". Apple was the first company to reach a $1 trillion valuation. Steve knew something about speaking out with courage when something needed to be said. So often we want to be popular, non-confronting, accepted. Yet it is only by challenging ourselves that we can do something aesthetically beautiful.

ENCOURAGING A CULTURE THAT'S TOO LAZY TO CLOCK ON TO BAD JOBS

Agile Manifesto Rule #10: Simplicity – the art of maximizing the amount of work not done – is essential.

Simplicity can and should drive everything for those who desire effective output. Leading agile teams means leading empowered teams. And specifically, teams that will not start something that smells wrong. Like a racehorse at the Grand National, a true thoroughbred refuses to jump when the fence is simply too high.

Many organizations and many leaders operate a top-down power culture. Top-down power cultures persuade people they should do what they are told or asked to do. They intimate that there are negative consequences for insubordination.

How can we get the best people, and get the best out of those people, if we then persuade them to start work on projects that are poorly designed, too complex or run by poor communicators? Simplicity dictates maximizing the amount of work not done. So why should we start something that will require extra work?

For many of us, this seems such a strong ideology that we can't envisage putting it into action. Could I really refuse to do something at work? Can I really say, "Folks, this smells wrong. Can we reevaluate?"

As with our Tuesday-night bike riders, simplicity evangelists are of huge value to teams. It's our job as leaders to promote bottom-up thinking, challenge at all levels and make huge calls about what not to do. Huge calls about what not to do are, more specifically, big challenges against something we are about to do! When put like that, it's not always so palatable.

As a consultancy, our company tries to be simple, easy to work with and effective. We explicitly make efforts to work for straightforward clients. There are no "hero calls" here for individuals who spend months managing a challenging client. Instead, we say, "Get out of there and find someone more fun to work with!" We have declined work and, at times, put the price up simply because the people involved seemed complex. Shock horror. Time is money. On the flipside, we have done some extraordinarily effective and low-cost work with highly collaborative, pragmatic and smart clients. Freelancers think the same way. How long is this actually going to take? How much pain is involved? What's all that worth?

Encouraging our team to think in this way helps us not to start bad jobs. It also encourages other parts of the business or clients to view time as the currency. To be easy to work with. To be clear.

At a governance level, simplicity strategies run hand in hand with the agile philosophy of short-term delivery of working products and getting work shipped. Collaboration strategies that prompt effective, challenging and responsive face-to-face meetings rather than complex political gaming.

In this way leadership is not really that difficult most of the time. Only occasionally. As chess champion Gary Kasparov says in his wonderful book *How Life Imitates Chess*, what is important is to understand how to "play our best chess in the most difficult moments".

SORT IT YOURSELF PLEASE

Agile Manifesto Rule #11: The best architectures, requirements and designs emerge from self-organizing teams.

I don't know about you, but when I look around my team I see a wide variety of individuals, each with different strengths.

Every individual has the capacity to lead, and at various moments, we all do. Psychological theory breaks down aspects of personality in one of two ways:

// "Type" is considered an unchangeable dimension of personality with varying strength.
// "Trait" is a set of behaviours on a spectrum.

There is no leadership type. Context, team composition, history and relationship strength all influence who is able to lead. A drawback with "type" approach to personality is the identity labels. Even the MBTI that proudly labels me as an extrovert acknowledges that I get a score on the introvert spectrum too. We all have the ability to lead. To what extent then does making "leader" an identity label help?

Imagine a team of ten people with a random composition of corporate people. It's likely that one or two characters have the natural disposition to take charge of the group. But what happens if we remove those people?

Time and again in my experience of the situation described above (we use it on leadership trainings), the group function improves as a result of removing the so-called leaders. Something in the dominant behaviour of these individuals diminishes other people's powers. So often the group function diminishes when someone takes the lead.

What's going on? Self-organizing teams are powerful. Very powerful. The unintended consequence of some leadership behaviour is that it blocks leading from others. It takes a great deal of self-awareness and attention to lead in a way that increases leading in others.

How do we do it? Here are some tips:

1. Keep saying it
Communication, communication, communication. "We want a team of leaders. This is an all-play environment. We encourage initiative at every level, I think you can handle this on your own" etc. Pick a few mantras and repeat it as frequently as Eurosport encourages me to purchase a Bora cooker extractor.

2. Push down responsibility
Allow all team members to lead various aspects of the organization. Share out the leading jobs. Allow junior staff to lead projects and have experienced staff work for them on the project without changing who is responsible.

3. Recognise leading
Positively reinforce leading behaviours. When people take initiative make a point of thanking them. Our recent placement student left wearing a captain's armband. A sign that we saw him leading in several areas.

4. Challenge senior people to delegate in bigger chunks
Why delegate a task when we can delegate the whole project? Do we really need to be involved in this? Big-chunk delegation makes it easier provided relationships are strong enough to offer support when any issues arise.

We may have to fire a couple of people to make space. But always, always, always (always) ensure attitude is the primary focus of the hiring process. Yes, their CV is extensive. Yes, they have done similar roles elsewhere. But anything less than a brilliant attitude dilutes the whole team. Find people who love leading. And hire them.

How to lead self-organizing teams

Recently I faced two challenging situations. Partly because each (IMHO) required different strategies for leadership.

// Scenario one was primarily a request for direction regarding team function and internal practice.
// Scenario two was a discussion about a piece of client work.

How did I lead in each of these scenarios?

The value of ambiguity

In scenario one, two of my colleagues wanted a decision made. It wasn't a clear-cut decision and there was plenty of ambiguity.

I like ambiguity. Ambiguity demands each of us to think about the best thing to do. Ambiguity promotes critical thinking and principle-centred decision-making. But ambiguity is a hard master, demanding constant attention. Ambiguity does not allow us to relax into rules. It constantly agitates us.

My internal monologue was asking my colleagues, "Do you want me to tell you what to do?" That would have been massively the easiest thing to do.

But, in order to reinforce the premise that "self-organizing" teams outperform "leader-led" teams (which we have built our business on), my strategy in this interaction was this: Let them work it out. Sometimes my job is to abdicate, disappear and decline.

Intrusive leadership

In scenario two, four of us were debating the optimum strategy for a client project. The Interactive Workshops crew is a highly intelligent community that is good at intellectual debate. This ten-minute discussion went on for two hours, spanning both a meeting room and, when we got booted out of there, the kitchen. The crux of our debate was this: To what extent to do we want to get into conflict with the client. This can be one of the trickiest aspects of consulting.

The debate raised a moral dilemma. The client asks for X, to achieve Y. But will X actually work? And will it achieve Y? What would you do? We can't ignore that money is a factor here. We could get paid to make X. We could make profit from making X. But what if we do it believing that X may not work, and that it won't achieve Y?

In this case, intrusive leadership was required. Forcing a debate. Forcing tough conversation and difficult questions. Yet, where possible, still not directing leadership. I wanted to lead my team to clarity; I didn't want to tell them what to do. This kind of leadership is more akin to academic debate or philosophical questioning. Jointly we came to some pretty cool strategies to work with the client to take the project to the next step. I think we were all happy with the outcome.

The analogy

In chess, one way to win is to offer your opponent bait. Sacrificing a piece, say your queen's pawn, that, when taken, sets in motion a chain of events and ultimately leads to your victory. The counter strategy by players who spot and resist the bait would be known as "queen's pawn declined".

Often, we can decline requests for leadership as part of a clear strategy. It may involve some "short term pain for long term gain". But, if we want a team full of leading, it's a strategy we will want to master. And this style of leadership is not an easy path. It's a daily choice.

SIMPLE STEPS IN CONTINUOUS IMPROVEMENT: EVEN BETTER IF

Agile Manifesto Rule #12: At regular intervals, the team reflects on how to become more effective, then tunes and adjusts its behaviour accordingly.

Leading a continuous culture is very, very simple. It starts with us. The infamous study on this by Zenger and Folkman leaves us with an unarguable chart. There is a direct positive correlation between employee engagement and the extent to which leaders give honest feedback in a helpful way.

Gives honest feedback in a helpful way

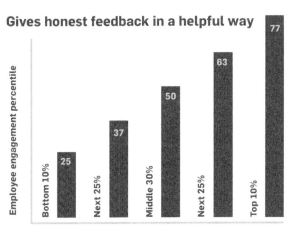

Employee engagement percentile

Bottom 10% — 25
Next 25% — 37
Middle 30% — 50
Next 25% — 63
Top 10% — 77

Gives honest feedback

But there is an even stronger emphasis on how frequently we as leaders seek feedback on how to improve. The more frequently we ask, "How can I improve?" the greater our teams perceive our leadership effectiveness (especially if we can actually act on their feedback, of course).

Actively looks for opportunities to get feedback and improve

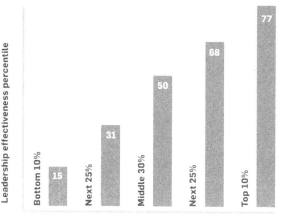

Looking for opportunities to get feedback

Leaders seeking feedback are open. They can say "yes" to doing something new. To growing. Yet the blocker is often our current well-honed habits and routines. To change these ingrained practices is to embrace unlearning...

Adventures in unlearning

Having dropped my kids at school recently one morning I headed to the office on the tube, arriving at 9:05 am. It was a new commute for me, and the culmination of six months of solid unlearning during which our team has hit stratospheric performance highs. This is what I believed six months previously:

// Homeworking is most efficient – we don't need an office
// I don't need a coach/advisor – we know what we
   are doing
// Monthly 1:1s are less effective than a walk around
   the park
// A five-day-a-week job in an office is dull
// I can leave the detail to someone else
// All we need to focus on is revenue/profit
// 50–60% growth will be very challenging
// Bottom-up management is the way to go
// Hire great people and everything else takes care of itself
// Email is for shmucks. Just text me.

My kids are avid unlearners. Their growth requires it. Stuff we teach them in certain phases – "hold my hand by the road", "don't climb the stairs alone", "it's time for your nap" – soon becomes irrelevant as they reach new levels of maturity. Not only are old lessons replaced with new ones, but also, by necessity, the foundational skills have to be unlearned. You can't walk to school safely alone AND hold my hand.

As a placement student at the Body Shop's world-class L&D department, I remember a fabulous Ashridge Business School article that described how, "the skills we need in our thirties are the opposite of the skills we need in our forties". I'm sure the study has been tidied up to remove age discrimination, but the essence is the same. Big-shift job changes tend to require the reverse set of skills to those that gave us our success.

Here are some examples:

//   In early career phases, competing against our peers
      helps us stand out and get promoted, but in later career
      phases competing against peers is what creates
      difficult politics. Senior people expect us to do our job,
      and respect them for doing theirs.

//   In early career phases, our personal skills and ability
      to get things done individually develop our capability and
      performance. In later career phases, unless we achieve
      results through others we become swamped and perform
      strategic aspects of our job at a low level.

//   In early career phases, it's okay to compromise a bit on
      work/life balance etc. and invest extra energy in work.
      In later career phases, we have greater life
      responsibilities, and getting this balance out of kilter
      undermines the meaning of work and life to the detriment
      of our mental health, relationships and family.

//   In early career phases, it's important to learn to work
      with the culture we are in. In later career phases, we
      have the responsibility for cultural leadership.

//   In early career phases, one year seems a long time.
      In later career phases, if we are only looking one year,
      ahead we may well derail.

At the end of the day, I sat in the office, after a full day with
our fabulous non-exec director, Karen, running 1:1s, on the
second day of a five-day week in the office, with a day of
detailed financial analysis ahead of me, which is all growth
focused, with a motivated team planning to do 100% year-
on-year growth from Karen's top-down target, planning to
carefully manage the great people we are hiring.

I still think email is still for shmucks. But when I've unlearned
that ... the transition into my next career phase
will be complete.

CONCLUSION

An agile mindset is for everybody. Not all the time. Just when it works. Whilst myriads of software teams have used agile over the last 15 or so years, it is only recently that other parts of organizations have caught up. The real secret is not the process. It's that the agile mentality can be a conduit for developing highly effective, delivery-focused teams. Many of the elements of the agile mentality correlate exactly with the fast-paced, empathy-driven, results-oriented culture of the best teams in business.

For those of us in teams, we can apply the principles in the manifesto and the attitudes and tactics in this book to our own work. I love the idea of delivering "working products as often as possible" to a manager. I love the idea of saying, "Change it, of course!" to Karen, our non-exec director. And I love the idea that, if we are really output focused, we can rebalance something that has been lost in 100+ years of industrialization. We are now all artisans. Somehow, getting the job done and getting home, or getting the job done from home and heading to the gym, school pick up or pub – that excites me. That's the freelancer's payoff. That's the reward we should all get for being effective. Not more work. Not longer hours. But choice.

Team leads in larger organizations have the power to supercharge culture. Turning a team agile is an awesome experience. Many current no-no's become yes-yes's. Rules can be bent. Shortcuts taken. Watching people who have been siloed become liberated. What a joy. Projects will certainly not work out "as planned". Maybe some will get canned. I hope so. Too much effort in the last 50 years has gone into outputting pure junk. We can be in the privileged position to positively benefit our teams lives, simply through sticking to some principles and processes. Or, as that guru Steven Covey put it in his first principle, and as I have shared simply with hundreds of leaders over the years: Starting, with the end in mind.

THANKS

I had no idea when I sat down over Christmas 1988 and started competing with my siblings at "Mavis Beacon Teaches Touch Typing" that in the summer of 2018 I would sit down over 14 days and write The Agile Secret. During these two intense weeks, I worked through five sprints against a very clear plan agreed by my fabulous editor Victoria over a brunch. The design team laid out the whole thing and sent it to print inside a week. If there is any urgency in the writing, that's the reason. We agreed that it didn't have to be perfect. It just had to be done.

Sprinkled across these pages are anecdotes from my experiences over 20 years in business, training over 10,000 executives at some of the world's most fabulous companies. You simply cannot work for Rolls-Royce, Airbus, Mercedes, Allen & Overy, BBC, Savills, CBRE, BAE Systems, HSBC, Morgan Stanley, Red Bull, Leica, Schindler, Spirax-Sarco Engineering, BNP Paribas, etc, or train executives from Coca-Cola, GSK, Pfizer or MINI without assimilating much tacit learning about the best ways to get things done.

Whilst working initially as a freelance trainer, as our company has grown, my understanding of what it takes to lead has changed. The best of what I learned as a trainer has been recycled and deployed as a leader. In some ways, leadership is much harder than the theory. In other ways, behind a fabulous team, leadership is a breeze.

Turns out writing a book is not that hard; if it's short, you have a lot to say for yourself, can touch type and have a massive support team.

The support team behind this project is long and distinguished. The key rocks in the jar are Steph, Annabelle, Joseph, Mum, Dad, Lizza and Ben. The whole Interactive Workshops crew over the years has been a laboratory and a playground for many test-flight crashes. Conkey, Steph, Charlie, Kat, Zöe, Jonny, Chris, Sophie, Shegun, Nathan, Simon, David, Pete, Johnny, Victoria, Mim, Karen, Emily, Susan, Chris, Rosie, Matteo and co. Plus freelancers too many to mention ... maybe apart from Crispin and Angela? And Hutch. And in the recent season, where I'm no longer on the frontline of agency life, a few very special clients that have let relationships go deeper: Ruth, Shaun, Kim, Jonathan, and others that have, as my closet "bosses", encouraged me to be a better leader and a better person.

I'm really excited to be in touch with anyone who wants to give feedback. If you do, the next book will be better!

Jonna
CEO
Interactive Workshops

Email: jonna@interactiveworkshops.com
Twitter: @jonnasercombe
LinkedIn: www.linkedin.com/in/jonnasercombe

ADVENTURE...

Every time you pause at reception,
take a swipe card and push your way
through the turnstile of a major global
organization there is something new to
learn. Scratching around the world with
not much more than a passport, a laptop
and a flipchart marker provides an
education no MBA can compete with.
I'd like to thank the following who,
perhaps just for a brief moment
invited us in.

Apologies if I forgot to return
the name badge.